Evangel-lies:
Lies Christians Believe About Evangelism

—⚜—

By Dr. Rob Peters

XULON PRESS

Copyright © 2007 by Dr. Rob Peters

Evangel-lies
by Dr. Rob Peters

Printed in the United States of America

ISBN 978-1-60266-051-9

All rights reserved solely by the author. The author guarantees all contents are original and do not infringe upon the legal rights of any other person or work. No part of this book may be reproduced in any form without the permission of the author. The views expressed in this book are not necessarily those of the publisher.

Unless otherwise indicated, Scripture is taken from the HOLY BIBLE, NEW INTERNATIONAL VERSION®. NIV®. Copyright © 1973, 1978, 1984 by International Bible Society. Used by permission of Zondervan. All rights reserved.

www.xulonpress.com

Dedication

Evangel-lies is dedicated to Drs. Ed and Kelly Guthrie. Ed, you are a pediatric ophthalmologist who is helping people really see.

Introduction

Most Christians and churches misunderstand evangelism. Examine the evangelistic efforts of most churches and you will discover that few people are involved and very little is accomplished. Most church members believe that evangelism is a job for a pastor or it is a program. The statistics on evangelism tell us that very few Christians "get it" when it comes to evangelism.

The Bible is very clear, however. Evangelism is not the job of a select few on special occasions. Instead, evangelism is the natural expression of a Christian who demonstrates a love for God by telling others how they can have hope, peace, and purpose in life through Jesus Christ. Telling others about God's love and forgiveness should be as natural as breathing for a believer. Jesus taught and the early church illustrated that evangelism is the primary work of the local church. Evangelism is not a program. It is a way of life. The key to the explosive growth of first century Christianity and the radical transformation of communities was mobilizing ordinary Christians to share the extraordinary story of God.

Pastors and theologians may unknowingly perpetuate the problem. Few pastors have exposed the ordinary laypeople found in the Bible who were responsible for the explosive growth of the early church. They, like most biblical commentators, overlook the heroes of evangelism found in the middle chapters of the book of Acts. It is the middle chapters of Acts that tell the story of the explosive growth and exciting passion of the early church. Most commentaries outline the book of Acts in two parts. Acts 1-12 develops the ministry of Peter, and Acts 13-28 describes the ministry of Paul.

Sandwiched between these prominent and professional preachers are the laymen who are the heroes of early church evangelism: Stephen, Philip, Ananias, and Cornelius. By unpacking the lives of these ordinary churchmen we discover examples of effective evangelism and are inspired to follow their example.

Evangel-lies is important for three reasons. First, it speaks to the majority of those who make up the church, the laymen. Most Christians will never receive professional training for ministry. Yet, it is the responsibility of ordinary Christians to share their story of salvation and the story of God's love and forgiveness with other people.

Second, lay-evangelism follows the biblical model for performing ministry. Pastors are not to do the work of the ministry so much as they are to train the people to do the work of the ministry (Ephesians

Evangel-lies

4:11-12). The church is severely hampered when it relies solely on the ministry and efforts of professional clergy. Mobilizing individual Christians to tell others about Christ has always been God's plan.

Third, we live in a day when the pastor can no longer go where he once could. He cannot go into the schools, the business center, or the government square. He must train his people to take the good news of the hope, peace, and purpose with them as they go to their offices, schools, and neighborhoods.

As a pastor I try to offer biblical truth in biblical language with appropriate biblical application. Therefore, I have chosen to address the topic of personal evangelism from the perspective of a biblical study of Acts 6-10. I will not address every issue within this text, but I do believe the central teaching of Acts 6-10 is lay-evangelism.

It is my ambition to provide a resource that is multi-functional. First, *Evangel-lies* offers pastors an expositional outline of Acts 6-10 along with illustrations to use when preaching on lay-evangelism.

Second, *Evangel-lies* is a great resource for small groups who need to focus on the how-to's of evangelism. *Evangel-lies* is divided into a four parts. Each story is told in a way to make the book useful as a small group Bible study. Each chapter concludes with discussion questions that will be helpful for a small group leader.

Third, *Evangel-lies* can also be used as a devotional guide for the layperson seeking to be equipped and inspired to share their faith in Christ with others. There are four chapters that are divided into sub-sections. Each of these sub-sections can be useful for a morning quiet time. The reader will find both biblical principles and application in each section.

If there is a benefit to be drawn from this work, I hope it will be to renew an interest in telling the story of salvation. If you learn something or are inspired, share it with others, practice it, and reproduce it.

I wish to thank my wife, Wendy, and my children, Anna Grace and John, for their contributions to this work. They are always patient, understanding, and honest as I sort through my experiences with God. You are each special, unique, and a wonderful gift from God.

I also wish to thank Paula Lonsway and Gail Raybould for their administrative support through out this project. Both of you are a gift from God and serve others above yourself. You are sacrificial and faithful as servants of God.

Finally, I wish to thank Dr. and Dr. Ed and Kelly Guthrie for their encouragement and financial support to make this book possible. You have been a blessing in my life. Thank you.

Chapter 1: Stephen
Acts 6:1–8:1

Can't Find the Post Office

A story is told in Billy Graham's *How to Be Born Again* about the author going to a city to preach an evangelistic crusade. He checked into his hotel, unpacked, and wrote several letters. After a long afternoon in the hotel, he decided to go for a walk. He thought he would find a place to mail the letters along the way. His short walk turned into a long walk when he did not find a mailbox or post office. He stopped a little boy on the street and asked, "Son, do you know where I can find the post office?"

The little boy replied, "Sure, Mister, just go down the road to the corner. It is on the other side of the street."

Mr. Graham thanked the boy and began to walk away. After taking a few steps Billy realized he had not invited the boy to come to the crusade that night. He wheeled around and shouted to the little boy, "By the way, son, I'm preaching at the stadium tonight, and I'd like you to come. I'm going to talk about how to get to heaven."

The little boy looked at him with a puzzled look and said, "Mister, if you don't know how to get to the post office, how in the world do you know how to get to heaven?"

Most of us feel that way when it comes to evangelism. We think, "How in the world, God, can You use me to tell someone else how to get to heaven?"

Define Evangelism

Most Christians never think about what evangelism really is. So let me define clearly what evangelism is. Evangelism is presenting Jesus Christ in the power of the Holy Spirit with the revelation of Scripture in such a way that sinful people repent and place their faith in God as they receive Jesus as Savior and allow Him to be the Lord of their life.

Let me show you how Stephen evangelized his community.

Stephen's Story

Stephen's story is the first of the four stories that transition the book of Acts from the story of Peter to the story of Paul. Peter and Paul are the two main characters in the book of Acts. But sandwiched between their stories Luke records the stories of four laymen.

It is important not to miss these four stories and to learn the lessons their lives teach. Stephen, Philip, Ananias, and Cornelius initiate the church's worldwide ministry and make an indispensable contribu-

Evangel-lies

tion to the church. These lesser-known characters facilitate the church's expansion and provide examples of how ordinary people can tell others about Jesus. Since Stephen's ministry served as a catalyst for the expansion of the church, let's consider his ministry first.

Stephen secured a place of significance by overcoming his fear of persecution and presenting a simple plan of salvation to his listeners. I want you to read these pages and remember Stephen was an ordinary layman. He learned how to talk to others about Jesus, and you can too. What does Stephen's story tell us about a person who shares the story of Jesus?

Acts 6:1–8:1 tells the story of Stephen in four parts. Luke describes Stephen's character (6:1-8), Stephen's challenge (6:8-15), Stephen's case (7:1-53), and Stephen's courage (7:54-8:1).

1. Stephen's Character

> In those days when the number of disciples was increasing, the Grecian Jews among them complained against the Hebraic Jews because their widows were being overlooked in the daily distribution of food. So the Twelve gathered all the disciples together and said, "It would not be right for us to neglect the ministry of the word of God in order to wait on tables. Brothers, choose seven men from among you who are known to be full of the Spirit and wisdom. We will turn this

Evangel-lies

responsibility over to them and will give our attention to prayer and the ministry of the word."

Philip, Procorus, Nicanor, Timon, Parmenas, and Nicolas from Antioch, a convert to This proposal pleased the whole group. They chose Stephen, a man full of faith and of the Holy Spirit; also Judaism. They presented these men to the apostles, who prayed and laid their hands on them.

So the word of God spread. The number of disciples in Jerusalem increased rapidly, and a large number of priests became obedient to the faith.

Now Stephen, a man full of God's grace and power, did great wonders and miraculous signs among the people.

Acts 6:1-8

We are introduced to Stephen because a dispute arose in the church. Stephen and six others were selected to serve in the administrative ministry of the church. The apostles wished to give their attention to preaching and praying, so Stephen and his team were named as the first deacon body. The early church's faith and confidence alone tells us a great deal about his character.

However, three phrases are added that more fully describe Stephen's character. Each phrase helps to

Evangel-lies

develop a more complete picture of Stephen's character. The Bible says he was "full of the Spirit and wisdom," he was "a man full of faith and of the Holy Spirit," and he was "a man full of God's grace and power."

Full of the Spirit and Wisdom

First, Stephen was said to be a man "full of the Holy Spirit and wisdom." Luke describes Stephen as a man who was both spiritual and practical. The Spirit is certainly given to every believer, but the phrase "full of the Spirit" describes a man who was faithfully under the control of the Spirit. The quality of being full of the Spirit, however, did not cause him to cease being practical. Luke counterbalanced this spiritual quality with a practical quality. As a pastor I have observed that some spiritual people don't have a practical bone in their body. I have heard these kinds of people described as "so spiritually-minded they are no earthly good." This cannot be said of Stephen. He was spiritual and practical.

The Hebrew concept of wisdom provides insight into Stephen's work of evangelism. Wisdom for the Hebrew was two-dimensional. It included both knowledge and application. Wisdom was never knowledge alone. Knowledge had to be applied to the situation one faced before it was considered wisdom. Effective evangelism requires both dimensions. Stephen exemplifies knowledge and the ability to apply this knowledge when he speaks about Christ.

Biblical knowledge is certainly required when a Christian shares their faith in Christ. At the close of this chapter we will learn five biblical facts that must be shared if anyone we tell about Jesus is going to truly be saved (lie #2). However, we must also demonstrate wisdom as we apply this knowledge to our interactions with people. Careless evangelism has appropriately been described as trying to pick fruit before it is ripe and casting your pearls before swine. Wisdom instead knows what to share and when to share it. Stephen's sensitivity to the Holy Spirit and his practical insight helped him be an effective witness for Christ.

Full of Faith and the Holy Spirit

Second, Stephen is said to be "full of faith and the Holy Spirit." Stephen yielded complete control of his life to God, and he believed God would work in him and through him. He was sensitive to God's activity and leading, and he was aware of God's presence.

Take special note of the word *faith*. It is an important word in our spiritual vocabulary. Stephen believed God. He took God at His word.

Let me ask you a very serious question: Do you have faith in God? You may say, "Yes, I have placed my faith in God." I am glad you have, but I am talking about having faith that God can change people's lives.

This is one of the most important components of Stephen's character that made him an effective witness. He really believed that God could change a person's life. He really believed a person could be saved and changed. He really believed that God could save the men who sat on the Sanhedrin. Even

Evangel-lies

though the Sanhedrin had sentenced Jesus to die and threatened the apostles, Stephen still believed God could save them. Do you? Do you think God can save the worst of sinners?

Before I return to this thought, notice that Stephen was right. The Bible records that "a large number of priests became obedient to the faith." I believe Stephen had been sharing his faith in Jesus with these men long before he made his final speech. He saw many of these men come to faith in Christ.

What does it mean to have faith when it comes to evangelism? It means you believe God can take the worst of sinners and, by His grace, transform them into the best of saints. Do you believe that? Do you believe that the worst of sinners in your community or family can be saved? Do you believe God can reach the most rebellious person, the worst of atheists, the most pronounced pagan that you ever have known?

I faced this question a number of years ago when I witnessed to a family member. He was a lifelong alcoholic who never demonstrated anything but contempt for Christ. He was an avowed atheist. I sat with him one day at the beach and shared my faith in Christ with him. I prayed for him and thought carefully about what to say. I mustered up the courage and began to tell him about Jesus.

I thought he would surely be convinced. After all, I did what God wanted me to do, and I did the best I knew how. All I got was a laugh. He laughed at me. I felt stupid, little, and insignificant. I could not believe it. How could God let this happen? I saw this man

Evangel-lies

over the course of the next several years, and I vowed to never talk about spiritual things with him again.

After several years passed I learned he was in the hospital in a very serious condition. Several times we thought he would die. My wife and I decided we needed to go and visit him. We needed to say goodbye to him and express our love to the family. We made the trip home and went to the hospital. I knew God wanted me to share Jesus with him again, but I just didn't want to be embarrassed again. I didn't want to be rejected. But I knew God wanted me to do it.

As we entered the room, he was sitting up. He recognized me. I was a little surprised he was so alert. After a little small talk, I started to talk about spiritual things. I was honest and acknowledged that he almost died. I told him I was concerned about him because I knew he was not ready to die. I shared with him that God created him and loved him. I told him his sins separated him from God, but that God had not stopped loving him. I told him how Jesus died for him and rose again from the grave. I described how good works could not save him, but that he could repent and place his faith in Jesus (see lie #3).

After sharing these five biblical principles, his wife unexpectedly gave her testimony. She told him what her life had been like before Christ, how she received Christ, and what Jesus had meant to her since. As I looked back, I noticed a tear well up in his eye. His lip began to quiver. He said, "I know I'm not ready to die. What do I need to do?" I asked him to pray with me, and he gave his life to Christ right there.

Evangel-lies

Let me ask the question again: Do you believe God can take the worst of sinners and transform them into the finest of saints? I must admit that sometimes my faith wavers. I wonder if God really can reach a person. Time and time again God has shown me that He and He alone can save and change a person. The issue is that we, as His children and His witnesses, must believe that God can do it. Do you have that kind of faith? If you do, it can move a mountain. If not, put down this book and pray for God to grow your faith and trust in Him.

Full of Grace and Power
Third, Stephen is said to be "a man full of God's grace and power." G. Campbell Morgan said of Stephen, "He was a man of sweetness and strength." He was gentle and gracious. Perhaps that was why he was chosen by the early church to work with widows. He was gracious towards these widows in the administration of the daily distribution of the bread. He was probably praying for them and encouraging them. He was gracious toward them just as he was toward those who did not yet know Christ.

Notice that grace is not weakness. We know this because he was also filled with power. It was obvious that the dynamic power of God was working within him. He was energized to work and speak on God's behalf. What a wonderful combination, a merging of the sweetness and the strength of God into one personality. This is a winsome combination. That is a wonderful thing—to be gracious without being passive and to be powerful without being offensive. He had blended into one personality the traits that made Jesus effective in encountering and engaging people.

We need these two character traits in our lives if we are going to be effective witnesses. We need this kind of balance and spiritual maturity. When our lives are marked with this kind of character, Christ-likeness is going to shine through in our interactions with other people.

Ponder these three qualities of Stephen's character and consider the impact these made on the people he met. Stephen was not a preacher, orator, or scholar. He was not skilled in persuasion or philosophy. He was not a student of famed rabbis. But he was a man of wisdom, faith, grace, and power. God was at work within him. He had a faithful and regular walk with Jesus.

You can have the same impact on the people God has placed in your life, but you must let God do in you what He did in Stephen. You must let God work in you so He can work through you. The more time Stephen spent with God, the more God was at work within him. The more contact you have with God, the more God will develop your heart. The point is this: the more God is at work in you, the more God will work through you.

Before I leave the discussion of Stephen's character take note that every Christian is called to ministry but not every ministry is the same. Stephen was asked to serve tables while the apostles preached and prayed. But notice that Stephen did not use his service in one area to prevent him from evangelizing.

Evangel-lies

I have observed as a pastor that most Christians look for a reason to not evangelize. They justify their thoughts by saying they don't have that spiritual gift, but that they will serve God by doing something else. This is not how God works. He expects everyone to use their gifts, skills, and calling as a platform to share our faith. Everyone is to evangelize. They are simply to use the ministry God has given them as a platform to do evangelism. Stephen did not use waiting on tables as an excuse for not evangelizing, and you should not and cannot use the ministry you have as an excuse for not telling others about Jesus. The ministry you have is simply the platform for sharing your faith in Jesus with others.

2. Stephen's Challenge

> Now Stephen, a man full of God's grace and power, did great wonders and miraculous signs among the people. Opposition arose, however, from the members of the Synagogue of the Freedmen (as it was called) - Jews of Cyrene and Alexandria as well as the provinces of Cilicia and Asia. These men began to argue with Stephen, but they could not stand up against his wisdom or the Spirit by whom he spoke. Then they secretly persuaded some men to say, "We have heard Stephen speak words of blasphemy against Moses and against God." So they stirred up the people and the elders and the teachers of the Law. They seized Stephen and brought him before

Evangel-lies

the Sanhedrin. They produced false witnesses, who testified, "This fellow never stops speaking against this holy place and against the Law. For we have heard him say that this Jesus of Nazareth will destroy this place and change the customs Moses handed down to us." All who were sitting in the Sanhedrin looked intently at Stephen, and they saw that his face of like the face of an angel.

Acts 6:8-15

Luke describes how Stephen faced a severe challenge. The Bible says, "Opposition arose." *Opposition* is another word for personalizing the persecution. Stephen experienced what everyone experiences when they try to share their faith: opposition. Someone told him to sit down, be quiet, and mind his own business. This is one of Satan's most effective intimidation tactics. Unfortunately it works very well.

The Bible says, "Everyone who lives a godly life in Christ Jesus will be persecuted" (2 Timothy 3:12). But Jesus reminds us, "Blessed are those who are persecuted because of righteousness, for theirs is the kingdom of heaven" (Matthew 5:10). These two verses should prepare every believer for the conflict that will follow when they begin to represent Christ.

Luke describes the confrontation in three short summaries that have similar parallels for our own life's experiences. First, Stephen was accused. The Synagogue of the Freedom began to gang up on Stephen. This particular synagogue was probably

Evangel-lies

comprised of disgruntled Jews who once were slaves, thus "freedmen," from the various regions mentioned. They challenged Stephen to a verbal sprawl. The altercation did not end the way they hoped. They did not know the kind of man they were messing with. The Bible says, "They could not stand up against his wisdom or the Spirit by whom he spoke." Stephen had an inspired wisdom. His adversaries found they could not match up against his arguments.

This is an important insight to remember when you think about giving a verbal witness. When you are telling someone about Jesus, God promises to "give you the words to speak" (Matthew 10:20). The words He gives you will be based on His heavenly wisdom that the Bible says, "is filled with the Spirit's power" (1 Corinthians 2:4).

God describes in 1 Corinthians 1 and 2 that the wisdom of man is foolishness compared to the wisdom of God and that in our weakness, the wisdom of God is revealed. I find tremendous comfort in these words. They tell me to trust God, open my mouth, and God will speak through me when I tell the story of Jesus. The weaker I feel, the more God will empower my words. So if you feel like a weakling when it comes to sharing Jesus, you may be in the best place to be effective at evangelism. You are in the right position to let the power of God work through you.

Paul's thoughts convey these ideas: "In my weakness I found the strength of God to be very present in my words, in my life, and in my message." And I don't know about you, but even as a seminary-trained pastor I find my greatest comfort and encouragement in these words. My experience tells me that if you ever feel fully equipped by yourself to share Jesus with others, you probably are not dependent on God the way you should be.

Second, Stephen's character was maligned. When they discovered they could not get the better of him through reasoned argument, they decided to descend into a smear campaign. They stirred up some bad characters and bribed them to lie about Stephen. This is usually what happens when debates are lost. The debate led to an argument that eventually turned into lies. It is not hard to understand why the lies and smear campaign did not work. When you are dealing with a man of Stephen's character, the mud usually does not stick.

Stephen was not looking for a fight. He was just defending the truth. People got mad about the truth. Mark this down. People who want to be rebellious towards God will always become angry and violent towards the truth and the one bearing the truth. Contrast this with the position that Christians take when sharing their faith in Christ with a nonbeliever. We are never to persecute another in order to force them to come to Christ. We are willing instead to be persecuted in order to promote the love of Christ and to demonstrate the convictions of our beliefs. This is significantly different than most religions in our world today. However, Christians can validate their faith by their willingness to suffer for what they believe.

Third, the Bible says they resorted to violence. They debated. They resorted to mud slinging. Finally, they resorted to violence. "The seized Stephen..."

Evangel-lies

The idea is that they dragged him away as if they intended to do violence to him. They produced false witnesses who said he had blasphemed against God. They accused him of threatening God's house and God's law.

The Jews have always been pretty sensitive about these two areas. They were interested in defending the law and the temple. These were their two most treasured possessions. These were the most sacred things to them. So they decided they would use these two sacred articles to bring charges against Stephen.

We know that Stephen was teaching in the exact tradition of Jesus when it came to the law and the temple. But just as Jesus was misunderstood, so was Stephen. Regarding the temple, Jesus taught that when the temple was destroyed, He would rebuild it in three days. Of course the teachers of the law were dismayed. It took forty-six years to build the temple. How could Jesus speak about rebuilding the temple in just three days? But the disciples knew Jesus was referring to His body because one greater than the temple was there (Matthew 12:6).

Second, regarding the law, Stephen was following Jesus' teaching that contradicted the scribal misinterpretations of Moses. They saw Jesus as a threat to the law even though Jesus had assured them not a single letter would be abolished of the law. Stephen was being portrayed in the same negative light as Jesus was. While his accusers were describing what he was against, the temple and the law, Stephen was about to describe what he was for. The case he presented emphasized he was for God's sovereign presence

Evangel-lies

over the entire world and a comprehensive interpretation of the law.

This is a very important lesson for those wishing to better share the story of God's love with others. We must always remember we are not just against things. Jesus is for things. We must be active as witnesses to describe what we are for. We are for changed lives. We are for holiness. We are for love, peace, and hope. We are for fulfillment and purpose. We are for marriages, families, and reconciliation. There is so much we are for, and there is so much Jesus can do. We need to do a better job describing how Jesus can change people's lives. Evangelism in this light can be seen as painting a picture for a person about how a new life in Jesus can create for them both a new eternity and a new earthly life.

Today, we should take heart from Stephen's story. We should not fear persecution. We should expect it. We need a change of mindset in order to understand that our persecution will be a part of what God uses to validate our message and nurture the faith of our listeners. Having this kind of Christ-like character overcomes rumors, hatred, bigotry, and anger. These are all squelched because the love, self-control, mercy, and peace of God are reflected in our lives.

Verse 15 describes how this works. They looked into Stephen's face, and it was like they were seeing an angel. What is the Bible saying? They could see God working in Stephen. Stephen overcame the severe challenge by letting the character of Christ radiate through his life. When we let the character of

Evangel-lies

Jesus shine through us people will see God at work in us, and this will draw them to Jesus.

Counterattack

As you read the story of the early church, you realize God had a game plan that carried the gospel from Jerusalem to Judea to Samaria and finally to the outermost parts of the world. Not long after God initiated His work, Satan began his counterattack. His counterattack was along three lines. Today Satan works along these same lines to prevent the church from evangelizing.

First, he uses intimidation. The disciples kept being brought before the Sanhedrin. They were warned to "stop preaching about Jesus." They were being intimidated. The goal of this intimidation was silence. Satan continues to use intimidation tactics to silence the church.

Second, Satan used corruption. Ananias and Sapphira's story is told in Acts 5. We are told for the first time believers in the church were morally corrupt. They claimed they sold all their property and gave the proceeds to the Lord, when in fact they only gave part of it to the Lord. They were lying, and moral corruption was endangering the testimony of the church.

Third, Satan uses distraction. In Acts 6 there was a fight within the church. People were complaining, "We're not getting our due, we're not getting enough of the resources, we're not getting enough in ministry." All of a sudden there was a distraction

Evangel-lies

from within the church, preventing it from going and sharing.

Satan doesn't want you to fulfill your responsibility to tell the story of salvation. He does not want you to be fishers of men. "Follow after me," Jesus said, "and I will make you a fisher of men." So, what does Satan do? He distracts the church. He corrupts the church. He intimidates the church. Today so many people's lives and so many of God's churches are in such bad shape that few people even evangelize. The only thing that will overcome these attacks is a Christ-like character.

3. Stephen's Case

> "Then the high priest asked him, 'Are these charges true?'"
>
> Acts 7:1

Two accusations are leveled against Stephen. The first charge was that he defiled the temple. The second charge was that he disregarded the law. Stephen answers the first charge about the temple by retracing the history of Israel. Stephen uses four of the most famous Jewish figures to conclude that God is not limited to the Holy of Holies in the Jewish temple. Regarding the second charge, Stephen defends himself against accusations that he disregarded the law by embracing a comprehensive view of the law. Stephen, in fact, defends the law against scribal misinterpretation. Observing how Stephen summa-

Evangel-lies

rizes these themes helps us learn valuable lessons about how to present the gospel to other people.

It is vitally important to remember Stephen's style of evangelism here. It is apologetic. I do not mean he is apologizing for what he has to say. I have heard many Christians who sound like they are apologizing when they speak about what Jesus has done for them. Instead, I am saying Stephen is offering a defense of the Christian faith by using carefully crafted arguments that help prove the reasonableness of the Christian faith.

In his marvelous work, *The Spirit, The Church, and The World*, John Stott quotes George Bernard Shaw and the commentator Diblius when they describe Stephen's speech as rambling, dull, incoherent, and lacking in interest and in point respectively. Many commentators try to defend Stephen's lengthy speech. I rather choose to take comfort in it. Anyone who has ever opened their mouth in front of a large group of people recognizes the dangers associated with public speaking. There is the danger of misquoting. There is the danger of rambling. There is the danger of inserting your foot into your mouth, as the old proverb goes. The reality is that Stephen delivers a wonderful case that was inspired by God, but it was not a perfect speech.

I take great comfort in knowing God used Stephen's best but less than perfect efforts. I believe Stephen was given the words to say just like Jesus promised his followers. I believe Stephen spoke with fear and trembling, just as Paul described his words to the Corinthian church. I believe this happened in order that Stephen's message might rely on the power of God, not the wisdom of men. I really believe our Christian witness would be a lot better and a lot more effective if it came naturally out of our head, hearts, and mouths under the inspiration of the Spirit.

I find that most believers in America today are so interested in controlling every area of their lives that they never leave room for God to work. I am not suggesting that we never study, prepare or consider our remarks. This would be a wrong response and out of balance too. What I am suggesting is that we turn the gospel loose and speak up for Christ without wondering if we can defend the gospel or not. After all, the gospel does not need us to defend it.

I like what Spurgeon said when asked how he defends the gospel. He said, "I don't need to defend a lion." Isn't that the truth? We need to do our best with what God has taught us and open our mouth and tell more people about what God can do in their lives. I will offer a suggestion at the close of this chapter under the heading *lie #3* that will help you understand the essential content of the gospel. But the greatest need is to tell the story of how God loved the world.

The Temple v2-50

Consider what Stephen says about the temple. Let's outline Stephen's thoughts by the characters he lists, Abraham in v2-8, Joseph in v9-19, Moses in v20-44, and then the father-son combination of David and Solomon in v45-50.

1. Abraham v2-8

> To this he replied: "Brothers and fathers, listen to me! The God of glory appeared to our father Abraham while he was still in Mesopotamia, before he lived in Haran. 'Leave your country and your people,' God said, 'and go to the land I will show you.' "So he left the land of the Chaldeans and settled in Haran. After the death of his father, God sent him to this land where you are now living. He gave him no inheritance here, not even a foot of ground. But God promised him that he and his descendants after him would possess the land, even though at that time Abraham had no child. God spoke to him in this way: 'Your descendants will be strangers in a country not their own, and they will be enslaved and mistreated four hundred years. But I will punish the nation they serve as slaves,' God said, 'and afterward they will come out of that country and worship me in this place.' Then he gave Abraham the covenant of circumcision. And Abraham became the father of Isaac and circumcised him eight days after his birth. Later Isaac became the father of Jacob, and Jacob became the father of the twelve patriarchs.
>
> Acts 7:2-8

The first of the four major epics that Stephen uses to make his case about the temple is a summary of

Evangel-lies

the life of Abraham. In his summary, Stephen makes the point that God is not a geographically limited God. God appeared to Abraham in Mesopotamia. This would have been inconceivable to the ancient person. Gods were considered to be geographically limited. The temples in each of these regions were believed to house the ancient deities.

Stephen challenges the Sanhedrin's thinking by describing how they were limiting the all-powerful God. They were limiting God's reach, His power, and His control. Stephen makes the case that God appeared to, spoke to, sent, promised, and rescued His people no matter where they were located. Stephen reminded the teachers of the law that God takes the initiative and involves Himself in the lives of His people no matter where they are. Stephen might have had Psalm 139:7 in mind. It says, "Where can I go from your Spirit? Where can I flee from your presence? If I go up to the heavens, you are there; if I make my bed in the depths, you are there."

2. Joseph v9-19

> Because the patriarchs were jealous of Joseph, they sold him as a slave into Egypt. But God was with him and rescued him from all his troubles. He gave Joseph wisdom and enabled him to gain the goodwill of Pharaoh king of Egypt; so he made him ruler over Egypt and all his palace.

Evangel-lies

Then a famine struck all Egypt and Canaan, bringing great suffering, and our fathers could not find food. When Jacob heard that there was grain in Egypt, he sent our fathers on their first visit. On their second visit, Joseph told his brothers who he was, and Pharaoh learned about Joseph's family. After this, Joseph sent for his father Jacob and his whole family, seventy-five in all. Then Jacob went down to Egypt, where he and our fathers died. Their bodies were brought back to Shechem and placed in the tomb that Abraham had bought from the sons of Hamor at Shechem for a certain sum of money.

As the time drew near for God to fulfill his promise to Abraham, the number of our people in Egypt greatly increased. Then another king, who knew nothing about Joseph, became ruler of Egypt. He dealt treacherously with our people and oppressed our forefathers by forcing them to throw out their newborn babies so that they would die.

Acts 7:9-19

The second of the four major epics Stephen uses to make his case is the story of Joseph. If God appearing in Mesopotamia was odd, God showing up in Egypt was extraordinary. God rescued the favored son of Jacob in what many Jews would have considered the home turf of their archenemy. What was even more amazing was that God never lost control

Evangel-lies

---

of Israel or the promises He made to Israel while they were there. God was able to use Egypt to rescue Israel from famine. He was able to provide for Israel and grow Israel into a nation while being cared for by the most dominant power in the world.

3. Moses v20-44

"At that time Moses was born, and he was no ordinary child. For three months he was cared for in his father's house. When he was placed outside, Pharaoh's daughter took him and brought him up as her own son. Moses was educated in all the wisdom of the Egyptians and was powerful in speech and action.

"When Moses was forty years old, he decided to visit his fellow Israelites. He saw one of them being mistreated by an Egyptian, so he went to his defense and avenged him by killing the Egyptian. Moses thought that his own people would realize that God was using him to rescue them, but they did not. The next day Moses came upon two Israelites who were fighting. He tried to reconcile them by saying, 'Men, you are brothers; why do you want to hurt each other?'

"But the man who was mistreating the other pushed Moses aside and said, 'Who made you ruler and judge over us? Do you want to kill me as you killed the Egyptian yesterday?'

Evangel-lies

When Moses heard this, he fled to Midian, where he settled as a foreigner and had two sons.

"After forty years had passed, an angel appeared to Moses in the flames of a burning bush in the desert near Mount Sinai. When he saw this, he was amazed at the sight. As he went over to look more closely, he heard the Lord's voice: 'I am the God of your fathers, the God of Abraham, Isaac and Jacob.' Moses trembled with fear and did not dare to look.

"Then the Lord said to him, 'Take off your sandals; the place where you are standing is holy ground. I have indeed seen the oppression of my people in Egypt. I have heard their groaning and have come down to set them free. Now come, I will send you back to Egypt.'

"This is the same Moses whom they had rejected with the words, 'Who made you ruler and judge?' He was sent to be their ruler and deliverer by God himself, through the angel who appeared to him in the bush. He led them out of Egypt and did wonders and miraculous signs in Egypt, at the Red Sea and for forty years in the desert.

"This is that Moses who told the Israelites, 'God will send you a prophet like me from

Evangel-lies

your own people.' He was in the assembly in the desert, with the angel who spoke to him on Mount Sinai, and with our fathers; and he received living words to pass on to us. But our fathers refused to obey him. Instead, they rejected him and in their hearts turned back to Egypt. They told Aaron, 'Make us gods who will go before us. As for this fellow Moses who led us out of Egypt—we don't know what has happened to him!' That was the time they made an idol in the form of a calf. They brought sacrifices to it and held a celebration in honor of what their hands had made. But God turned away and gave them over to the worship of the heavenly bodies. This agrees with what is written in the book of the prophets:

"'Did you bring me sacrifices and offerings forty years in the desert, O house of Israel?
You have lifted up the shrine of Molech
and the star of your god Rephan,
the idols you made to worship.
Therefore I will send you into exile' beyond Babylon.

"Our forefathers had the tabernacle of the Testimony with them in the desert. It had been made as God directed Moses, according to the pattern he had seen.

Acts 7:20-44

Evangel-lies

The third epic is the longest retelling of the story. In the story, Moses is born, raised, trained, expelled, called, and used to rescue the people of Israel from Egypt. Emphasis is again placed upon the fact that God was not geographically limited. He spoke to Moses even in the wilderness. The place where God met with Moses was called holy ground. Moses returned to Egypt to lead his people out of bondage in the power of God after having failed to lead them out in his own power earlier in life. God was able to overcome the strongest military force on earth at the time to free His people. He defeated Ra, the sun god, and his earthly embodiment, Pharaoh. God again met with Israel in the desert at the Holy Mountain. He gave them the law, and the people entered a covenant relationship with God.

4. David and Solomon v45-50

Having received the tabernacle, our fathers under Joshua brought it with them when they took the land from the nations God drove out before them. It remained in the land until the time of David, who enjoyed God's favor and asked that he might provide a dwelling place for the God of Jacob. But it was Solomon who built the house for him.

However, the Most High does not live in houses made by men. As the prophet says:
"'Heaven is my throne,
and the earth is my footstool.

>What kind of house will you build for me?
>says the Lord.
>Or where will my resting place be?
>Has not my hand made all these things?'
>>Acts 7:45-50

Finally, Stephen speaks about David and Solomon. David and Solomon are listed as the monarchs who prepare for and construct the first temple that replaced the tabernacle. Even these men who led the construction effort of the great temple did not fall into the trap of limiting God in power or in scope. They recognized that God "does not live in a temple like a man lives in a house" (Acts 7:48).

Stephen certainly makes his point clear even if he does not make it concise. God's presence is not limited to any particular place. God is advancing His kingdom, and He calls His people to follow Him in new and exciting experiences. God is a God who is with His people. God is a God who has made it possible to be with His people through Jesus.

When we evangelize we would do well to remember this. God is not limited. God is able to go to people. God wants to get involved with people. God is active and engaged in our world. God is a God who pursues.

The Law

Stephen shifts his attention to address the second issue the Sanhedrin challenged:

Evangel-lies

> "You stiff-necked people, with uncircumcised hearts and ears! You are just like your fathers: You always resist the Holy Spirit! Was there ever a prophet your fathers did not persecute? They even killed those who predicted the coming of the Righteous One. And now you have betrayed and murdered him—you who have received the law that was put into effect through angels but have not obeyed it."
>
> Acts 7:51-53

Stephen addresses the second accusation leveled against him. He speaks about the accusations regarding the law. His defense is that he was more biblical than those who accused him. He puts his accusers on the defensive. Stephen communicates respect for the law. He has already acknowledged Moses' divine calling and work. God had been in charge of all the events of Moses' life, including giving the law to Israel. Stephen's problem with the teachers of the law was that they were not obeying what they called as precious. Stephen claimed that Jesus' interpretation of the law was rightly given. We find this in the Sermon on the Mount, where Jesus interprets six of the Ten Commandments with a fuller and deeper meaning than the scribes did.

Before we join the stoning party and cast our own stones in the direction of the Sanhedrin, let's consider our own lives carefully. I have never been in a Bible-believing church that did not consider the good news of Jesus' life, death, and resurrection as precious. But I have been in plenty of churches that have failed

Evangel-lies

to do anything significant with this precious story of salvation.

The reality is that many of us are just as guilty of doing with the gospel what Stephen accused the Sanhedrin of doing with the law. The Sanhedrin kept the law and eventually perverted it. Like it or not many Christians and many churches are doing the same thing with the gospel. God intends the gospel to be given and shared, period. I know many churches that are organized, relevant, administrated, and delegated, but they are missing the point. They are not reaching people. They say that the gospel is precious, but they will not lift a single finger to advance it. Jesus pronounced seven woes on the scribes and Pharisees for doing the same things. So before we cast a stone, we had better be sure we are faithfully giving the gospel away.

I heard a story about the German army and a man who had been wounded in battle. He goes into the hospital by order of his commander. He is being processed at the hospital and, to his surprise, he finds there are two doors in front of him. One has a sign that says "slightly wounded" and the other sign says "seriously wounded." He goes through the slightly wounded door. He gets to two more doors after a long corridor. One says "officers" and the other says "non-officers," so he enters the latter. He goes down another long corridor and gets to another set of doors and. When he gets there, it says "party members" and "non-party members." He goes through the non-party members' door only to look around and realize

Evangel-lies

he's been ushered right out of the hospital onto the street.

He later writes his mother and says, "Well, I went to the hospital."

She writes back and says, "Well, how did it go?"

He writes back to her and says "Boy, they have the greatest organization in the world, but nobody there ever helped me."

That's sometimes the way many churches are. We get all the organization in place, but we miss the point of helping the hurting people. And what is it that God wants to do with the hurting people? He wants to heal their hearts, and all of that begins with the gospel presentation. No life is really changed until Jesus is born into their heart.

Conclusion to Stephen's Case

Stephen made a compelling case. Notice I didn't say he made a clear case. I didn't say he made a concise case. I didn't say he made a good presentation. As a matter of fact, critics of chapter seven of the book of Acts say that he rambles, he chases rabbits, and he's difficult to follow. I say he sounds like a lot of us who are out there trying to share the gospel. What a fantastic thing to do. He actually tells the story of Jesus. This is more than most Christians will ever do. He is making a difference. He is in the battle. He is giving his life for something that matters.

4. Stephen's Courage

What was the result of Stephen's faithful witness? Let's just say it didn't go well. What? You mean he

Evangel-lies

obeyed God, honored God, did his best for God, and didn't get a prize? No, sometimes it doesn't work that way. Sometimes we do something good and only get punished for it. As the old proverb says, "No good deed goes unpunished." One of the great fallacies of the Christian faith is that when you do the right thing, everything turns out right. Listen to how things went for Stephen:

> When they heard this, they were furious and gnashed their teeth at him. But Stephen, full of the Holy Spirit, looked up to heaven and saw the glory of God, and Jesus standing at the right hand of God. "Look," he said, "I see heaven open and the Son of Man standing at the right hand of God."
>
> At this they covered their ears and, yelling at the top of their voices, they all rushed at him, dragged him out of the city and began to stone him. Meanwhile, the witnesses laid their clothes at the feet of a young man named Saul.
>
> While they were stoning him, Stephen prayed, "Lord Jesus, receive my spirit." Then he fell on his knees and cried out, "Lord, do not hold this sin against them." When he had said this, he fell asleep.
>
> And Saul was there, giving approval to his death.
>
> Acts 7:54-8:1

Evangel-lies

Stephen's selfless and fearless proclamation of the gospel led him to pay the ultimate price. He is known today as the first Christian martyr. When Stephen died, the church grieved for a man who was well loved. It also was scattered for fear of the same persecution happening to others. Yet, as they were scattered, they remained faithful and continued to share Jesus with others wherever they went.

Stephen's death was so much like Jesus' death. First, the angry Sanhedrin stoned Stephen the way they had called for Jesus' death. They rushed him and stoned him. As they did, Luke recounts that heaven opened and Jesus was standing at the Father's side waiting to receive him. Jesus stood to receive Stephen into heaven. He became the first one clothed in white standing before God's throne in heaven (Revelation 7:9-14). Jesus stood to confess Stephen before the Father in heaven just the way Stephen had been confessing Christ upon earth.

Second, Stephen committed his spirit to Jesus. He ask Jesus to receive his spirit the way Jesus had asked the Father to receive His.

Third, Stephen asked God not to hold these men accountable for his death. Even in death at the hands of evil men, Stephen granted them his forgiveness. At this, Stephen closed his eyes and fell asleep. Could there be a more beautiful description of his death? With stones raining down, Stephen had peace enough to fall asleep and awaken in heaven to the rich reward for his obedience.

Many people today around the world are dying for their testimonies. Yet here in America Jesus is asking us to live for Him. While many are dying around the world for speaking about Jesus, here in America many can't find the words or the courage to speak about Christ. Why is that? I believe there are three lies Stephen's story exposes that prevent Christians from sharing their faith in Christ. We need to expose these lies and examine ourselves to see if we have bought into ideas that prevent us from sharing our faith in Christ with others.

Lie #1: I would evangelize, but no one cares what I think.

This lie causes Christians to doubt their significance, reputation, and influence.

Significance

The question of significance is something everyone faces. We all ask ourselves the following: Do I matter? Can I make a difference? In our day, many people have a bad self-image. Some people think too much of themselves, but most people think too little of themselves when it comes to their spiritual identity. Our nation has embraced a humanistic philosophy of life. We therefore think of ourselves as merely animals. This thinking has serious deteriorated the value of man in man's eyes. God's value of man has not changed. God still thinks of man as the crown jewel of His creation. God says of man that it was a good creation, indicating that God was pleased with what He had made. Even after the fall of mankind, God still loves and cherishes His children.

God thought of man so much that from the very beginning God determined He would pay the ultimate price to demonstrate His love for people: He would offer His Son as a sacrifice for our sins. He did this because He cherished the people He created. He cherishes every person. He cherishes you. This leads us to only one conclusion: you matter to God. Because you matter to Him, God has a plan for your life. God has a purpose for your being in this world. God has something for you to do that no one else can do. That is significant, and when you know God and follow His plan for your life, you learn you are significant. This does not lead you to become proud. As a matter of fact, the exact opposite happens. You become humble. You come to the place where you understand that you should humble yourself to God and offer your life to God to fulfill the purposes He has for you.

Reputation

Many Christians are overly concerned about what others think of them. This is especially true when it comes to sharing our faith in Christ with another person. We ask ourselves, either consciously or unconsciously, what this person will think of us. This kind of thinking indicates wrong thinking. It is not Christian thinking or biblical thinking. When we ask questions like this or think thoughts like this, we are acknowledging that we are more concerned about what people think about us than what God is thinking about us.

Evangel-lies

America has become so self-aware that we struggle to demonstrate authentic Christian living. While the Bible does teach us to live in a way where we have a good reputation, it does not teach us to live in a way the world will ever fully understand. The Bible teaches us to live in a way that is respectable and winsome. We know that there will be things that will seem extremely strange to unbelievers (i.e. spending Sunday at church, giving money to missions, reading an ancient book to discover truth). As a pastor, I observe Christians who are more concerned about what others think of them than practicing their faith. What we need to do as Christians is live to please God, while being aware of how our actions, attitudes, and ideas affect others.

Influence

Jesus taught His followers that they should be salt and light in a tasteless and dark world. Jesus teaches people to use their influence to make the world a better place. Jesus taught people to influence the world. He wanted to use them to make the world a more moral place (salt). He wanted to use them to make the world a more spiritual place (light).

There are three primary qualities about salt that make it useful. Salt is stable. The chemical make up of salt is such that it is not easily broken down. Salt is tasty. It adds flavor to the food it seasons. Salt is a preservative. It prevents decay. Jesus uses this metaphor to describe the work of a believer. Christians should live stable lives that add flavor to the world

Evangel-lies

by offering spiritual influence that makes the world a better place.

It must be mentioned also that too much salt can be destructive and too little salt can be meaningless. Too much salt corrodes. It ruins and destroys the tastes. Lot's wife symbolized the latter. She had become so worldly that she chose the things of the world over spiritual things. Learning to shake just enough salt at just the right time is a very important skill.

Jesus also taught His followers to be light. Jesus taught people to shine their light corporately. He says, "A city on a hill cannot be hidden." Jesus' point is that the church community should always shine its light corporately as it preaches the gospel.

Jesus next describes the light of the individual. He says, "light a lamp . . . and put it on a lamp stand." Jesus wants His followers to shine their light before others so they can see God in us. We do this best when we share our faith in God with others. We certainly perform other deeds to earn the right to share Jesus with people, but all of the effort must lead to a verbal witness that testifies about the love God has for people.

Finally, Jesus teaches us to shine our light actively through our good deeds so they will praise God in heaven. The idea is that believers should shine their light before men through their attitude, actions, and activity.

Let me refer back to Stephen to illustrate my point. Everyone wanted to know what Stephen thought. Stephen was gracious, powerful, faithful, and wise. People respected Stephen, and he did not

Evangel-lies

let that go to his head. People could see God at work in Stephen, so they wanted to know what Stephen had to say. This is influence. Stephen's character provided him many opportunities to share his faith.

This principle can transfer over to you, too. The more God works in you, the more God will work through you. What do I mean by working in you? I mean God working His Word into your life. I mean spending time in prayer with God. I mean becoming sensitive to the Spirit through prayer. I mean learning knowledge and wisdom and patience as the Spirit of Jesus matures you. When you are growing like this, God is going to work through you.

The more you love God, the more you're going to love people. The more you love God the more you're going to see how you can be involved in people's lives. The more you're reading your Bible, the more you're going to say "I desire to be obedient because I realize what God has done for me." The more you pray and say "Holy Spirit, please open my eyes and guide me and my interaction and relationships with other people." The more you're going to yield to the Spirit's control when the Lord does open your eyes.

If you are living in the flesh, you're going to be hard and selfish. You will find yourself half-hearted and powerless when it comes to sharing Jesus. So evangelism begins long before you are standing before someone to share your faith. It begins when you let God work in your life so He can work through you. That means "being" comes before "doing." You must be with God before you go and work for God.

Evangel-lies

Your evangelistic efforts or lack of effort may be one of the barometers of your own spiritual condition.

Jesus taught this principle in the Sermon on the Mount, Jesus gave the Beatitudes before He commanded us to be salt and light. Many Christians never understand significance, reputation and influence. Stephen's life was a significant life. He discovered his significance in relationship to Jesus. He put his reputation on the line. He exerted all his influence to bring people to Jesus.

Lie #2: I would evangelize, but I don't want to be persecuted.

No one wishes to face the kind of persecution Stephen did, but Jesus promised that anyone who followed Him would face persecution. The persecution, however, can feel more intense when you are trying to tell others about Jesus. I think this persecution hurts worse because our effort is to try and help another person spiritually.

Try something and see if it is not true. If you read this book and determine that God wants you to share your faith with others, make a commitment to do it. I can assure you that the moment you get serious about telling others how they can have peace in life through the gift of salvation that Jesus offers, you will face persecution. The moment you ratchet up your intentions to evangelize, Satan is going to ratchet up his efforts to prevent you from sharing Jesus with someone else.

Satan is not concerned about you living a mediocre Christian life, but the moment you get serious about taking people to heaven with you, you have his attention. His goal is to keep you going along happy and lukewarm and unconcerned about others. The minute another person is on your heart to influence them for Christ is the minute all hell will break loose to prevent you from making a difference. Satan's tactics will be much like the Sanhedrin's tactics. He will accuse, lie, and cause violence in order to intimidate you. There are two kinds of intimidations you may experience, external and internal.

External

The first is what I call external intimidation. This kind of intimidation in America today is coming in the form of political correctness. We are told it's politically incorrect to mention the name of Jesus. It is politically incorrect to pray in Jesus' name. It is politically incorrect to claim Jesus is the only way to heaven. It is politically incorrect to claim America was founded as a Christian nation. You get my point.

The goal of those who use these kinds of intimidation tactics is to isolate Christianity to the fringes of society. Christians are being painted as radicals and extremists. If Christians can be made out as extremists, then our point of view can be dismissed without even ever being considered. This is what Satan wants. He wants to destroy our Christian witness and influence. He wants to kill our Christian nation. He wants to steal our Christian heritage.

Christians must remember that as we respond in this hostile environment, we must not give in to the enemy's tactics. This will do nothing but cause

Evangel-lies

Christians to lose their credibility. Christians must return hate with love. We must turn the other cheek. We must seek to convert our enemy, not just secure a verbal win. Christians must enter the arena of public interaction without wearing our feelings on our sleeve and not only stand up for but also share the faith we say we believe in. We must love others when they hate us and seek their good when they desire our destruction. We're not the first generation of Christians to deal with intimidation.

Internal

The second kind of intimidation is internal intimidation. When Satan gets a hold of us, we say, "Well, I don't want to be disliked by that person. I want them to like me. I don't want to hurt their feelings. I don't want to cause them any pain or have a painful encounter that might sever our relationship or make our relationship difficult."

I would remind you that whenever there is iron sharpening, sparks are going to fly. And because sin is a reality, when we talk about sin in the lives of others, sparks are going to fly. And I can assure you that you will have to overcome the challenge of the internal feelings about a desire to be liked as you try to share Jesus with others.

The desire to be liked is especially strong in a narcissistic society. The only thing that will overcome this internal fear is love. We are taught that love is the greatest thing in the world. It is greater than faith or even hope. Love casts out all fears Paul taught us. The kind of love the Bible describes is

God-like love. It is sacrificial love. It is selfless love. This kind of love never measures the cost of what it gives. It only gives in relation to how God has given. If God so loved the world and gave His only Son, how can we not give our time, talent, treasure, and testimony to Him?

Lie # 3. I would evangelize, but I don't know what to say.

Let me ask you a challenging question: do you like Jesus? Are you interested in spiritual things? If you are, chances are you will talk about your faith. We all talk about things we like or are interested in. Why is it then that most Christians do not talk about their salvation? One of the excuses people give for not telling others about Jesus is that they don't know what to say.

As I said in the introduction, there are five foundational truths that you must share in order to lead someone to Christ. The first is that God created and loves you. The second is that sin separates you from the relationship God intends you to have with Him. Third, God does not stop loving you when you sin; He sent Jesus to die and rise again so that your sins might be forgiven. Fourth, you cannot do enough good works in order to go to heaven. Finally, you must repent of your sin and place your faith in Jesus in order to be saved. Let me address each of these briefly and offer you a Scripture you can use to show this to someone else.

Evangel-lies

God Loves You

The most well-known verse in the Bible is John 3:16. It says, "God so loved the world that He gave His only son that whosoever believes in Him will not perish but have everlasting life." You will not get much of an argument from people on this point. They want to think that God loves them, but don't underestimate the power of someone hearing the words, "God loves you." I remember the first time I said that to someone. I did not expect the response I got. They cried. Most people don't feel loved. Most people rarely hear the words "God loves you." When they consider that God loves them, it is a warm and wonderful experience, especially when it is a kind and compassionate Christian who speaks it.

Sin Separates You

If the words "God loves you" warm your heart, the word *sin* will cut you to the bone. Sin is the taboo word in the American vocabulary. No one likes to think of sin. We hate the word so much we have redefined the concept. Yet the Bible is very clear. Sin is the most basic problem a person has. Sin is described in the Bible as missing the mark, irreverence, transgression, iniquity, rebellion, treachery, and perversion. The Bible also tells us that it leaves people feeling restless, guilty, and troubled. The Bible is very clear that sin offends God, affects the sinner, and impacts others. Romans 3:23 probably says it best and most simply: "All have sinned and fall, short of the glory of God." Romans 6:23 drives home how significant the problem of sin is. It says, "The wages of sin is death."

Jesus Died for You

Love and sin describe the good news and the bad news respectively. The best news, however, is that God did not stop loving people when they sinned. Romans 5:8 says, "But God demonstrated His love for us that while we were yet sinners, Christ died for us." When Paul summed up the good news of Jesus for the Corinthian church, he said Jesus lived, died, was buried, and rose again. I would encourage you to make it that simple in your interaction with people.

I personally believe that many pastors and many programs make the message more complicated than God made it. God made it simple and powerful. Jesus died in our place and rose again, promising those who repented and believed that they would have their relationship with God restored and enjoy eternal life in heaven. It is just that simple. To make it more complicated is to rely on man's wisdom, not God's.

I am not saying that there are not finer points of theology that are important. What I am saying is that those points can be better understood later by people who are filled with the Holy Spirit. There may be the occasional intellectual who has objections or needs greater theological insights. But that is not the case with most people God is convicting of sin and convincing that Jesus was who He said He was.

Works Won't Save You

This is an important part of the gospel presentation. I used to only mention this briefly when sharing my faith. Recently, however, I discovered that 99 percent of people I talked to about Jesus believed

Evangel-lies

they would go to heaven because they did good works. The Bible is clear in Ephesians 2:8-9: "It is by grace you are saved through faith, not of works, lest any man boast." Most people think they can earn their way into heaven. They believe either their good deeds outweigh their bad deeds or that they are better than most people, therefore, God is under some kind of obligation to let them into heaven.

It is important to share with people that God is a perfectly holy God. He cannot even look upon sin. Therefore, even one sin makes us unable to share eternity with God. The only remedy for our sin is to either be punished ourselves or have someone take the punishment for us. That is what Jesus did. He took the punishment.

You Must Repent and Believe

There are both positive and negative issues to deal with here. Many people only deal with the positive side, believing that is enough. It is not. Some argue that the apostles, preachers, or even Jesus Himself taught that faith but not repentance was required to be born again. I will concede that there are some places in Scripture where certain people are not asked to repent, they are only asked to believe. However, a careful reading of these Scriptures reveals a repentant heart already existed.

Take, for instance, the woman at the well. She only needed to believe. Why? She already confessed to Jesus she had five husbands and was living with a man she was not married to. She acknowledged her sin. So when Jesus spoke to her, He talked about believing in

Evangel-lies

the Messiah. Romans 10:9-10 describes both of the biblical requirements for salvation, repentance and faith. The Bible says, "If you confess with your mouth that Jesus is Lord and believe in your heart that God has raised Him from the dead you will be saved." To address faith without repentance is to only preach half a gospel, which is really no gospel at all.

Conclusion

Let me close this chapter by offering several suggestions. First, mark the verses mentioned above in your Bible with a yellow highlighter. This will make them easy to find and easy to read if a person asks you to see them.

Second, always be ready to tell your testimony. This should be your spiritual life story. You can tell the one-minute version, the three-minute version, or the ten-minute version. Whichever you have the opportunity to share, remember to tell what your life was like before you knew Jesus, what it was like to come to know Jesus, and what your life was like after you experienced new life in Jesus.

Third, remember you will never be fully prepared to answer every question a person may have about God, Jesus, sin, and salvation. You are not there to defend what God has done, just to testify that God did it for you and describe how God can do it for another person, too.

Finally, let me tell you that the first time you talk to someone about Jesus you will think you did a terrible job. You might feel like you let God down or that the person you shared with will never know

Evangel-lies

Jesus because of how poorly you did. These are the thoughts Satan plants in your mind. God is so proud of you when you take the time and trouble to share Jesus with another person He loves. Don't worry if you did make some mistakes, because you will do better the next time. The more you share Jesus, the better you're going to become in telling God's story of salvation.

Jack Canfield tells the story "I'll Always Be There for You!" in his book *Chicken Soup for the Soul*. It's a fascinating story that comes out of the 1989 earthquake that almost flattened Armenia. This deadly tremor killed more than thirty thousand people in less than four minutes. In the midst of all the confusion of the earthquake, a father rushed to his son's school. When he arrived there, he discovered the building was flat as a pancake.

Standing there looking at what was left of the school, the father remembered a promise he made to his son: "No matter what, I'll always be there for you!" Tears began to fill his eyes. It looked like a hopeless situation, but he could not take his mind off his promise.

Remembering that his son's classroom was in the back right corner of the building, the father rushed there and started digging through the rubble. As he was digging, other grieving parents arrived, clutching their hearts and saying, "My son! My daughter!" They tried to pull him off what was left of the school, saying, "It's too late! They're dead! You can't help! Go home!" Even a police officer and a firefighter told him he should go home.

To everyone who tried to stop him he said, "Are you going to help me now?" They did not answer him, and he continued digging for his son stone by stone.

He needed to know whether his boy was alive or dead. This man dug for eight hours and then twelve and then twenty-four and then thirty-six. Finally in the thirty-eighth hour, he heard his son's voice as he pulled back a boulder. He screamed his son's name, and a voice answered him.

"Dad? It's me, Dad!" Then the boy added these priceless words: "I told the other kids not to worry. I told them that if you were alive, you'd save me. When you saved me, they'd be saved, too. You promised that, Dad. 'No matter what,' you said, 'I'll always be there for you!' And here you are, Dad. You kept your promise!"

Study Questions

1. Discuss ways your character and conduct can benefit the way you present the story of salvation not detract from it.

2. Discuss the challenges you feel when you try to talk about Jesus.

3. Discuss each of the five parts of the gospel presentation after you reread the Bible verses.

4. Discuss how you can overcome your fear to tell others about Christ by focusing on God's love.

Evangel-lies

Activities:

1. Write out your personal testimony in three parts. Describe what your life was like before Christ. Tell how you came to faith in Christ. Conclude by describing how God has changed your life.

2. Use your hand to account for each of the five parts of the gospel found in Lie #3 and practice them until you no longer need the book to remember them.

Chapter 2: Philip
Acts 8:4-40

Perhaps the single greatest miracle that God has worked in the world in the last hundred years is the miracle of the Chinese church's growth. In 1949, China became a communist country, and in 1950 the churches were shut down. The missionaries were expelled. Pastors were no longer allowed to minister, and seminaries could no longer operate. A few registered churches were allowed to operate if they conceded to government regulation. The government controlled the sermons preached and the ministries performed.

The China Inland Mission, one of the most well-known missionary organizations in the world, recorded at the time the churches came under government control that 986,400 Christians lived in China. Astoundingly, conservative estimates of the number of Christians in China today is somewhere between sixty and eighty million. Think about it. No seminaries. No church facilities. No pastors. No advertising. No evangelism. Few Bibles. After more than forty years of government control, the church doubled in size six times. That is a miracle. My takeaway is that so many of the programs and skills that the American church relies upon to reach people are not as necessary as we think. In fact, they may be the very things that prevent us from experiencing explosive growth in the American church.

The underground Chinese church has established their next goal: to organize another one hundred thousand underground churches with one hundred members in every church. Can you imagine the revolution that is taking place? It makes you wonder if the best church growth strategy wouldn't be to fire all the pastors, close all the seminaries, and watch our churches grow.

What caused the church to grow? We would certainly say that it was, first and foremost, the Lord. Secondly, I would say that the members of the church understood very clearly their responsibility to do the work of the ministry. They understood and obeyed the biblical method for performing ministry. Pastors teach and train people and the people go and do the ministry.

It is shocking and scary to compare America with China. In China the laypeople are serving and sharing within the church naturally, relationally, and obediently. Yet in America, Dr. D. James Kennedy's ministry, Evangelism Explosion, surveyed and concluded that 95 percent of American Christians never share their faith. The George Barna Group of Ventura, California, says that fewer than 10 percent of American Christians even feel any obligation to

Evangel-lies

share their faith. In other words, they just don't feel like it's their responsibility. It's not something that they are supposed to do. Is it any wonder that there are twice as many unchurched people in America today as there were just a generation ago?

We know God wants people to be saved. The question is how does God reach those who do not know Him? Some people have the misconception that evangelism is the pastor's job or the responsibility of those involved in an evangelism program at church. They miss the fact that evangelism is every believer's responsibility. Enter Philip. His story describes how God uses ordinary Christians and different styles of evangelism to reach a variety of people for Christ.

Mass Evangelism

> Those who had been scattered preached the word wherever they went. Philip went down to a city in Samaria and proclaimed the Christ there. When the crowds heard Philip and saw the miraculous signs he did, they all paid close attention to what he said. With shrieks, evil spirits came out of many, and many paralytics and cripples were healed. So there was great joy in that city.
>
> Acts 8:4-8

Philip's story follows on the heels of Stephen's stoning. After Stephen was stoned, the early church faced heavy persecution. Saul who witnessed the death of Stephen made it his ambition to destroy

Evangel-lies

the church. So with cruelty and passion he began to make life hard on these new Christ followers. When the persecution began, the apostles remained in Jerusalem, but the members of the church began to scatter throughout Judea and Samaria. The persecution caused the dispersion, but the dispersion did not stall evangelism. It resulted in greater evangelism. The pattern of evangelism followed the path Jesus had predicted—Jerusalem, Judea, and then Samaria.

As a pastor, I take special note that it was the people not the pastors who took the message of Christ with them. The Bible says they "preached the Word." This does not imply that they became professional preachers or filled traditional pulpits. They simply shared the good news about Jesus wherever they went. This is what Jesus commanded the disciples to do. They were commanded, "Go therefore into all the world and preach the gospel" (Matthew 28:19).

It is wonderful to see these early Christians obey the Lord. You cannot help but take note of how their obedience brought about God's blessing in their effort. They were not easily deterred from telling others about Jesus. They made no excuses for why they could not share Jesus. They overcame many threats and faithfully shared Jesus with others.

Philip's story is told as a trilogy. A trilogy is a message that is contained in a three-part story. The story is tied together with some common theme or sequence. Philip's trilogy is tied together by the theme of evangelism. Each story describes a different type of evangelism. Each effort was unique. Each story

Evangel-lies

demonstrates how Philip used a different style of evangelism to reach different people for Christ.

The first story describes how Philip evangelized a city through mass evangelism. The second story describes how Philip evangelized within the church by inviting people into the church to hear the gospel. The third story describes how Philip practiced personal evangelism as he shared Christ with a man he met on the road to Egypt. Philip's three stories help us understand that God cares about all people and uses different styles of evangelism to reach different kinds of people.

Philip Was a Layman

Philip, like Stephen, was a new deacon in the early church. As a layman, he did not leave all the preaching to the apostles. He was not afraid to speak up and tell others about Jesus. One of the misconceptions that laypeople have in the twenty-first century is that you must be a pastor and have a church or pulpit to preach. This is a lie that many believe. Acts 8:4 counters this lie. It teaches that "those who... preached the word" were not preaching formal sermons in traditional churches. Instead, it conveys the idea that the people shared the story of Jesus' life, death, and resurrection as they fled Jerusalem and wherever they sought refuge.

Philip Was a Minister

Philip was nothing more than an amateur missionary. However, he understood as a follower of Jesus that evangelism was to be a part of his life.

Evangel-lies

Two words enter the Christian vocabulary in Acts 8 that verify this truth. Acts 8 popularizes the word *evangelize*. It is used no less than five times (v. 4, 12, 25, 35, and 40). Reading these verses makes you conclude there is a message to convey, a messenger to convey it, and a recipient to receive the message. Philip was a layman who understood he had a message to share, and he made it his mission in life to share it.

The second word is *proclaim* (8:5). This word means "to herald." Philip became the herald for Jesus. He wanted to announce that Jesus was the Savior of the world to anyone who would listen. Philip understood that wherever he went he took Jesus with him. Therefore, he would try to introduce Jesus to everyone he met as if Jesus were present with him. When I take someone with me to a meeting or fellowship, I always introduce him to the other people present. In the same way when Jesus goes with us in our heart and life, we must introduce them to one another. This is out of both courtesy and respect.

It is also worth noting that Philip had a ministry in the church. He, like Stephen, waited tables as a deacon. He had a ministry and performed it faithfully. Notice, however, that his ministry became the platform for his evangelism, not an excuse for not evangelizing. Many of you reading this book already have a ministry. Perhaps because you have so compartmentalized your Christian life, you cannot see how the ministry you perform affords you opportunities to share Jesus with others. I ask you to reconsider your thinking on the subject.

Evangel-lies

God has given you your ministry in order that you can have opportunity to tell others about Jesus. Let me give you an example. When I worked at a church while in seminary I had the responsibility to visit hospitals. I compartmentalized my ministry so much that all I could think about was getting by to see all of my people. I never stopped to consider why God might have me in those hospitals in Dallas.

One day I met someone who actually asked me for help. While I assisted them, I was thinking about one thing. Getting back to "my" ministry. The Holy Spirit came on me so strong in that hospital and made me realize I was missing the whole point. I was there to complete my ministry assignment, but God had me there as a minister. I asked the person I was helping if they knew Jesus. They responded they knew the name, but not much else. I shared Jesus with them, and they came to faith in Christ.

I left that hospital a different person. I realized that while I was doing ministry God wanted me to use that platform to talk to people about their need for Him. Don't make the same mistake I made. Be like Philip. Use your place of ministry to share Jesus with those you meet and come in contact with. You will bring joy to your ministry and joy to the people you minister to, just like Philip brought joy to Samaria (Acts 8:8).

Philip Evangelized in Unexpected Places

Philip's first effort at evangelism took place in hostile territory. The Jews hated the Samaritans. The hostilities began more than one thousand years earlier when the kingdom was divided in the tenth century. Solomon's reign ended, and the kingdom of Israel divided under his sons. Later, the northern tribes were conquered and foreigners repopulated the Northern Kingdom after the Assyrian captivity.

The schism reached its apex when the Samaritans built a rival temple on Mt. Gerizim. The Jews considered the Samaritans half-breeds because they had intermarried with the Gentiles during their captivity. They established their own worship practices and rejected all the Old Testament except for the Pentateuch. In short, the Jews despised the Samaritans for both religious and racial issues.

The Early Church's Thoughts About the Samaritans

The early church evidently continued to think of the Samaritans in a degrading fashion. John asked Jesus to call down destruction on Samaria. The early church was so surprised when they heard about the conversion of the Samaritans that they sent their two leading apostles, Peter and John, to determine if they had really believed in Jesus and been saved.

Yet we should not be surprised at the Samaritans' response to the gospel. Jesus told His followers at His ascension that they were to be His witnesses in Jerusalem, Judea, Samaria, and the uttermost part of the world. Philip would be the one who saw this very prophecy be fulfilled. Jesus prepared His followers for their expanded ministry into Samaria. He journeyed into Samaria for one of His most notable encounters. On another occasion He told a parable

Evangel-lies

about a Good Samaritan. Jesus had really come to seek and save those who were lost, no matter what their race, nationality, creed, or gender.

The Samaritans were believed to be far away from God because of their false beliefs about God, worship, and the law. Samaria was the central headquarters for heretics. A heretic is someone who has a non-biblical doctrine, and the Samaritans certainly had different ideas than the Jews. They had established their own quasi-pagan religion, quasi-Jewish religion. But Philip went there and had startling results. Crowds gathered. The people listened. Philip saw God work miracles. The people responded to his invitation to repent and believe in Jesus.

Let's pause for a moment and ask an honest question. Do you believe Jesus can reach people who are far away from Him? Do you believe Jesus can reach the heretic, the atheist, and the antagonist? Philip did, and God can. Today in your community there are people who are involved in false religions and no religion. God wants to use you to reach them. They may be Mormons, Jehovah's Witnesses, Wiccans, Satanists, pagan worshippers, or atheists. Yet God loves them and wants to use you to reach out to them.

Consider what the Bible says about the kind of evangelism Philip practiced. Philip's initial efforts in Samaria might be labeled mass evangelism or crusade evangelism today. Crowds gathered. We are not told how large the crowds were, but we know it was a pretty big crowd by the word that was chosen to describe it. We are fairly certain that Philip was in the capital city of Samaria. We know this because

Evangel-lies

the Bible says Philip went to "The city in the region of Samaria." This was a common way of referring to the most important city in a region that is usually the capital.

So Philip went into the capital city in the region of Samaria and began to talk about Jesus. Before long, a crowd gathered. Philip, a layman, did not pass up the opportunity to share the story of Jesus' life, death, and resurrection.

In America we are familiar with this kind of evangelism through the ministry of Billy Graham and other less popular but nonetheless nationally known preachers. Yet, Philip was an ordinary layman. I don't know what took Philip to Samaria. Maybe he was setting up his new business after being expelled from Jerusalem because of the persecution. Maybe he was there to stay with family or friends until things settled down back in Jerusalem. Maybe the Holy Spirit led him there. Whatever it was that caused him to be in Samaria, he understood his responsibility to share Jesus with people wherever He was.

Have you noticed America is changing? You don't have to look very far or for very long before you realize Christianity is no longer the dominant influence in America. America does not reflect Christian values and beliefs like it once did. America does not allow Christianity in the public square or schools like it once did. The point I am making is that there are more people than ever before who need to hear about Jesus in America. More people than ever before have not heard the name of Jesus or the good news of what Jesus did to forgive them of their sins and change

Evangel-lies

their lives. More people than ever before have not been exposed to a Christian belief system.

We live in a day of opportunity when it comes to evangelism. The opportunity is there for ordinary Christians to open their mouth and tell others about Jesus. Notice again that verse 4 says, "Wherever they went...they proclaimed Christ there." I have heard many Christian people say they just try to be a good example in their workplace. And that's good. Your life ought to match your message. But, friend, I can assure you that unless you open your mouth and speak the words of the story of God, people are never going to understand how to give their life to Jesus Christ. Your life has to match your message, but your voice has to be used to speak the good news.

Luke adds one final word of motivation for sharing the story. Verse 8 says, "Joy comes to the city." Why? Because joy comes to the city that is evangelized. We live in a hopeless time. There is no peace; at best, there is temporary peace. But Jesus brings real peace, lasting peace. The Bible says that Jesus brings joy— a true happiness. Not just a shallow feeling of good emotions, but a joy that is rooted in God. The Bible says Andrew was filled with joy when he brought Peter to the Lord. That's why Zacchaeus, the Bible records, experienced joy when he was liberated from his financial pursuits and found Jesus. That's why in the parable of the Pearl of Great Price the man was pleased to sell everything he had in order to pursue the gospel message that brought hope and peace. The bridesmaids were happy when they were invited to go into the wedding feast. There is nothing as joyful

Evangel-lies

as telling somebody about Jesus. Philip had that experience by taking those who were considered the most horrible offenders of the religion and saw them experience the joy of the new birth in Christ when he shared Jesus with them.

Church Evangelism

> Now for some time a man named Simon had practiced sorcery in the city and amazed all the people of Samaria. He boasted that he was someone great, and all the people, both high and low, gave him their attention and exclaimed, "This man is the divine power known as the Great Power." They followed him because he had amazed them for a long time with his magic. But when they believed Philip as he preached the good news of the kingdom of God and the name of Jesus Christ, they were baptized, both men and women. Simon himself believed and was baptized. And he followed Philip everywhere, astonished by the great signs and miracles he saw.
>
> When the apostles in Jerusalem heard that Samaria had accepted the word of God, they sent Peter and John to them. When they arrived, they prayed for them that they might receive the Holy Spirit, because the Holy Spirit had not yet come upon any of them; they had simply been baptized into the name of the Lord Jesus. Then Peter and John placed

Evangel-lies

their hands on them, and they received the Holy Spirit.

When Simon saw that the Spirit was given at the laying on of the apostles' hands, he offered them money and said, "Give me also this ability so that everyone on whom I lay my hands may receive the Holy Spirit."

Peter answered: "May your money perish with you, because you thought you could buy the gift of God with money! You have no part or share in this ministry, because your heart is not right before God. Repent of this wickedness and pray to the Lord. Perhaps he will forgive you for having such a thought in your heart. For I see that you are full of bitterness and captive to sin."

Then Simon answered, "Pray to the Lord for me so that nothing you have said may happen to me."

When they had testified and proclaimed the word of the Lord, Peter and John returned to Jerusalem, preaching the gospel in many Samaritan villages.

Acts 8:9-25

In the first part of Philip's trilogy Philip used mass evangelism to tell others about Jesus. In part two he uses church evangelism to reach people for

Evangel-lies

Christ. Philip had many converts and no church, so he did what every missionary does. He started a church. We know from verse 12 that a church was started because Philip baptized these new believers. Baptism is a very significant Christian practice.

Let me digress to pursue one important thought. Many twenty-first century churchgoers have become accustomed to a public invitation being given at the end of a church service or an evangelistic event. As a matter of fact, we have grown so accustomed to this fixture in our service that it is considered sacred in many churches. We must recognize, however, that the early church did not extend a public invitation to respond to the gospel presentation. Instead, they used another method. It is the biblical method. It is baptism. It is the ordinance that Jesus asked His church to use in order to identify those who trust in Him.

Baptism accomplished many things. First, it identified new believers. They identified with Christ by being buried with Christ in His death and being raised to live a new life. They acknowledged that their sin was symbolically being washed away. Water baptism symbolically demonstrated how Jesus' blood washed away the sins in a person's life when they repented and believed. Believers were identifying with a new group—the church—when they were baptized. The point is that baptism has always been the biblical way of identifying those who have repented and believed in Jesus Christ. When we see these converts being baptized in verse 12, we know a church was being established.

Evangel-lies

Whenever a church begins to meet for worship, people begin to visit to find out what is going on. In verse 13 we learn that an unusual person heard about the church Philip started and came to hear Peter and John as they instructed these new believers. The visitor's name was Simon. He came to the church and heard the message and said that he believed in Jesus.

After fifteen years in ministry, I have learned this reality: if lost people aren't in the church service, no one gets saved in the church service. That is stating the obvious of course. However, we need to be reminded that when unbelievers come to church, they experience many things that draw them to God.

In 1 Corinthians 14:24-25 Paul describes the compelling experience an unbeliever has when they visit the church. The Bible teaches that the Holy Spirit will be at work convicting them of their sin and convincing them that Jesus can save them. They will experience the presence of a loving and holy God that assists them in understanding who God is and what He is like. In a Bible-teaching church they will hear the truth of God's Word that pierces their heart. In an evangelistic church they will have an opportunity to respond to the gospel. They will observe the loving fellowship of God's people and the wisdom and power of God's Word. All of these things have a significant impact on unbelievers when they come to church. But all of this only happens if they come.

Understanding that all of these good things happen when unbelievers come to church, we should do our very best to bring unbelievers to church with

Evangel-lies

us. Andy Stanley popularized the phrase "invest and invite," but it has been used before. These three words can describe how you can be used to share Jesus with others. You invest in their lives and use that investment as an opportunity to invite them to church.

More than 90 percent of Americans surveyed said they would go to church with a friend if they were invited. When people go to church they expect to hear about spiritual things. Therefore, you have the opportunity to participate in evangelism by simply living a good life in front of people and using your influence to invite them to church so they can hear your pastor tell them about love, forgiveness, and peace.

This kind of evangelism does not release you from opening your mouth and sharing Jesus with others yourself, but it does provide you another way to begin a conversation about spiritual things. The pastor's message can provide you the opportunity to ask your friend what they thought of the pastor's message. The door is just that wide open.

Simon the Sorcerer

Simon was an impressive and imposing figure in the city of Samaria. Simon is referred to as "the Sorcerer." He was known to work black magic and witchcraft and performed many great acts of magic that amazed the people. He impressed the people, but it was obvious that Satan was at work in him, not God. He is portrayed as an influential figure in Samaria. He heard about what Philip was doing, and someone probably invited him to attend Philip's service to see firsthand what was going on.

Evangel-lies

Let's make two observations about Simon. First, God specializes in reaching people that are living in absolute darkness. Many Christians believe it is easier to speak with someone who is nominally interested in spiritual things than someone who is seemingly opposed to spiritual things. I have found the exact opposite to be true. I have discovered that the further someone is away from God in lifestyle, attitude, and spiritual practices, the easier it is to share with them openly about God. I have found them to be much more open to the gospel than perhaps a moral person, or a spiritual person, or even a person who occasionally attends church.

My experience is that a little bit of light makes a bigger difference in a darker room than in a partially lit room. In other words, a Christian witness, testimony, or invitation usually does more good and is more powerful when given to someone we think might be unreachable. A person who is very sinful and lives a life contrary to the ways of God is often amazingly open to hearing about how God can change their life. That is why we must never believe the lie Satan whispers in our ears—that they will not respond to Christ.

Faith that Does Not Save

Second, Simon's conversion wasn't authentic. We don't know how Philip came to know about Simon's profession of faith in Jesus. Maybe he raised his hand in church. Maybe he requested to be baptized. Maybe he came forward after the service

Evangel-lies

was over. Whatever it was, he gave some indication of his belief in Jesus Christ.

Of course, for many of the people who were following Simon and participating in occult activity, their conversion was authentic. Simon's, however, was a false conversion. Verse 13 indicates Simon made some kind of profession of faith and began to follow Philip around. Luke writes in such a way as to indicate Simon took special notice of the great signs and wonders Philip performed.

When the report of what happened in Samaria reached Jerusalem, the church sent Peter and John to investigate. They found that Philip had preached a true and accurate gospel. The people had repented and believed. They had been baptized by immersion. Yet the Holy Spirit had not yet come upon them.

This part of the story requires an additional explanation. The question is does the Holy Spirit come upon a person when they are saved or is there an additional blessing that comes in the form of "the baptism of the Holy Spirit"? In *The Spirit the Church and the World*, John Stott gives a complete description of this passage.

Let me summarize his argument with three thoughts. First, the gospel had not yet spread outside of the nation of Israel, so when Philip preached the gospel to the Samaritans there was some question about whether or not they could really come to Christ. Second, Peter and John laid their hands on the new believers. They witnessed the coming of the Holy Spirit. Peter and John verified for the church in Jerusalem that the Samaritans really did receive

Evangel-lies

Jesus. Third, it is a dangerous practice to take the exception and create a rule out of it. Therefore, this passage where the Holy Spirit comes as a second blessing should not be standardized and should not therefore override the standard biblical norm of the salvation and receiving the Holy Spirit at the time of repentance and belief.

Maybe the simplest way to say it is that God withheld the blessing of the Holy Spirit in order to avoid a division in the church. Therefore, the apostles could confirm the salvation of the Samaritans and unite the church.

The story concludes with the apostles Peter and John laying their hands on these new Samaritan believers as the Holy Spirit comes upon them. When Simon saw this, he wanted the same ability to confer the Spirit on others. He wanted this gift so badly he offered money to get it.

Peter challenged him on three fronts. First, he excommunicated him (v. 21). Second, he called on him to repent (v. 22). Third, he identified his sin of bitterness (v. 23). In verse 24, Simon confesses that he couldn't even pray when he asked Peter to pray for him. Simon outwardly did what was required to follow Christ, but inwardly was never converted.

This is another caution for those who share their faith in Christ. Many believe that everyone who prays to receive Christ is saved. The truth is that not every person who indicates they are converted is really converted. Remember that not everyone who raises his or her hand, comes forward, or gets baptized is really saved. Only God knows who truly is saved.

Evangel-lies

Our responsibility is to faithfully witness to others about what Jesus has done for them, and one of the best ways is to take them to church with you.

Relationship Evangelism

> Now an angel of the Lord said to Philip, "Go south to the road—the desert road—that goes down from Jerusalem to Gaza." So he started out, and on his way he met an Ethiopian eunuch, an important official in charge of all the treasury of Candace, queen of the Ethiopians. This man had gone to Jerusalem to worship, and on his way home was sitting in his chariot reading the book of Isaiah the prophet. The Spirit told Philip, "Go to that chariot and stay near it."
>
> Then Philip ran up to the chariot and heard the man reading Isaiah the prophet. "Do you understand what you are reading?" Philip asked.
>
> "How can I," he said, "unless someone explains it to me?" So he invited Philip to come up and sit with him.
>
> The eunuch was reading this passage of Scripture:
> "He was led like a sheep to the slaughter,

Evangel-lies

and as a lamb before the shearer is
silent,
so he did not open his mouth.
In his humiliation he was deprived of
justice.
Who can speak of his descendants?
For his life was taken from the
earth."

The eunuch asked Philip, "Tell me, please, who is the prophet talking about, himself or someone else?" Then Philip began with that very passage of Scripture and told him the good news about Jesus.

As they traveled along the road, they came to some water and the eunuch said, "Look, here is water. Why shouldn't I be baptized?" And he gave orders to stop the chariot. Then both Philip and the eunuch went down into the water and Philip baptized him. When they came up out of the water, the Spirit of the Lord suddenly took Philip away, and the eunuch did not see him again, but went on his way rejoicing.

Acts 8:26-39

If Samaria represented those who were doctrinally far from God, Ethiopia represented those who were geographically far from God. Ethiopia was the outer boundary of the known world. Philip did not actually go there. Instead, the Spirit of God led him

Evangel-lies

to a place where he met someone. This is a good lesson. You may never go to the far corners of the world, but you can impact the world. If you have the opportunity to interact with and share the gospel with others, do it. You may be sending a missionary out into the world.

The story is set on a road in Gaza where an Ethiopian eunuch was returning home from worshipping in Jerusalem. He was probably a Jewish convert dispersed abroad. The Lord instructed Philip to "Go to the south road—the desert road—that goes down from Jerusalem to Gaza."

Philip obeyed the Lord. What was he doing? He was being sensitive to the Spirit. The Spirit of God was urging him to do something. The Spirit of the Lord was opening a door, and Philip obeyed. If God did that for Philip, He will do the same for you. Philip was sensitive towards God's leadership, and God opened the door.

I regularly hear another lie from Christians about evangelism. They say, "God has never led me to share Christ with anyone." If you have ever spoken those words as a believer, you should reconsider your definition of the word *led*, and you should make sure your heart is able to feel. God is always interested in reaching people, and He has made His existing followers ambassadors for Him (2 Corinthians 5:20). He is using us to communicate the message. He is leading you to do it. The question is to whom is God leading you?

Philip was being used to reach the eunuch through a personal relationship. This is the third type of evan-

Evangel-lies

gelism that is described in Philip's trilogy on evangelism. This one-on-one evangelism, or relational evangelism, is my favorite. I also believe that in the twenty-first century this type of evangelism will be the church's most effective strategy. The reason this relationship evangelism is so effective is that it tends to be the most authentic.

Perhaps the greatest turn off to our evangelistic efforts in the twenty-first century is a lack of authenticity. People are looking for that which is real. Jesus most perfectly modeled authenticity, and the church can effectively speak its message when it is authentic.

Jesus' authenticity is one of His most appealing qualities, but the inauthenticity of many Christians and churches is one reason why some people do not want to hear our message. When evangelizing, we must demonstrate four qualities if we are going to be authentic. These are four qualities Philip models for us.

First, our evangelism must be marked by sensitivity. The Bible says Philip ran beside the chariot the Ethiopian was riding in (v. 29). He placed himself in a position to have a conversation with this man. He did not force the conversation. He looked for the opportunity to enter into a dialogue with him.

Relationship evangelism is about entering into a conversation with another person about who God is, what God has done, and how they can receive the blessings and benefits of God's love for them. Today, conversations are more productive than lectures. Some may feel like having a dialogue with an unbeliever may impugn their faith in some way. A Christian dialogue with another implies neither a denial of the uniqueness of Christ, nor any loss of one's own commitment to Him. Instead, it allows a Christian to be genuine, humble, personal, and relevant. This kind of sensitivity when approaching an unbeliever can open lines of communication for honest dialogue.

Second, when we talk with unbelievers we must share our humanity. By this I mean we must demonstrate our own failures. If we just shout our message at people, our authenticity is questioned. Those listening do not know us, and for all they know we may be a phony or hypocrite.

When we sit alongside them and share our life and God's message with them like Philip did with the Ethiopian (v. 31), the relationship is authentic and personal. Defenses come down. We begin to be seen for what we are—sinful, needy, and equally dependent upon the grace of God. Not only are we known, but we also begin to know. We see others as human beings with sins, pains, frustrations, and convictions. We begin to feel their pains, and we want to share the good news with them because we care.

Third, when we converse with people about Christ, we must speak with humility. Philip started where the man was. He was reading Isaiah. He did not understand what he was reading, and Philip began where he was and answered his questions. We do not know the entire conversation, but we do know Philip was approachable, humble, and non-threatening, otherwise he would not have been invited to ride in the chariot.

Maybe it is humility that better equips Christians to share with others what Jesus has done for them. Humility is an attractive quality and draws people to us. What is it about humility that draws people? I think humility attracts people because it does not parade itself around in arrogance like the rest of the world. It does not act superior in attitude or words. After all, many people reject Christ because they have seen in us or in other Christians a caricature of Christ that makes Him unappealing. Our desire when we evangelize cannot be to score points or win a victory, but instead to share what God has shared with us.

Finally, when we converse with a person about Christ, we must demonstrate integrity. Philip did this by testifying to the truth about Jesus and letting the chips fall where they may. Philip started where the eunuch was and testified about Jesus (v35). Verse 36 indicates that some time passed as they traveled along. Philip did not know where the conversation would conclude. He simply spoke the truth in a loving way to the man God brought across his path.

We must engage people in the same way. We must honestly pursue truth wherever it leads, even if it reveals inherent weakness in our faith, lifestyle, or character. We must avoid stereotypes and fixed formulas with predetermined destinations. We must follow the lead of the Holy Spirit and address the real needs of our friends.

This kind of authentic interaction is winsome. It invites our conversationalist into a relationship.

When a person sees the love, security, and support of a Christian person, they can see within the church what they are looking for—love, acceptance, and community. Developing and maintaining authentic relationships will make us more effective in our evangelistic efforts.

Faith that Saves

The Ethiopian eunuch's story ends with his baptism. Again, this is where an authentic profession of faith is best made. The eunuch requested baptism, and Philip obliged. The story concludes with Philip being taken away by the Spirit, but not before another life was changed.

We see Philip doing mass evangelism, church evangelism, and personal evangelism. Do you get the idea that evangelism is important? Do you understand you can do evangelism in many ways? Do you get the idea that Jesus had it right when he said, "Leave the ninety-nine to go and reach the one"? Evangelism is the priority. It is essential. Philip certainly understood this, and we should as well.

Let me make one more observation about Philip before we list additional lies Christians believe about evangelism that prevent them from sharing their faith. No one was off Philip's radar screen when it came to evangelism. Philip witnessed to the ordinary person and the extraordinary person. There was no one too high on the socio-economic scale, and there was no one too low on the socio-economic scale. Philip saw all people the same. He saw them like God sees them. This might best be termed *redemptive compas-*

Evangel-lies

sion. Redemptive compassion is not seeing someone as the world sees them, but it is seeing them for what they can become in Christ Jesus.

All people need to be forgiven of sin and provided with hope. We should keep this clear in our minds as we seek to share Jesus. I often see Christians involved in evangelism programs who feel like they can give something to people who are lower on the socio-economic scale than they are. I believe this is because they feel superior to them. There is almost condescension in their evangelistic efforts. I would guard carefully against this tendency. This is not a Christ-like attitude.

Philip models for us exactly how we should practice evangelism. We share with all people, knowing they all have sinned and fallen short of the glory of God. What was said of Jesus could be said of Philip, and we should pray that it could be said of each of us. Matthew 22:16 says, "Teacher, you're no respecter of men because you pay no attention to who they are." That meant that Jesus could go up the scale of the socioeconomic system as well as down. He treated the one at the bottom the same as the one at the top. He treated the one in the middle the same as the one at the bottom or the top. He knew all people were the same at the core of their being.

So we see how Philip preached to the masses, spoke in the church, and shared with individuals. He was willing to reach all people from all places. Let's use this story to address three additional lies Satan tries to make us believe to keep us from sharing our faith in Christ.

Lie #4: I would evangelize, but that's the pastor's job.

I have often heard this lie in my own church, but I flatly reject it. It is not biblical. The Bible plainly says God called "some to be pastors and teachers, to prepare God's people for works of service, so that the body of Christ may be built up" (Ephesians 4:11-12).

This does not imply that pastors are not to share their faith. They should. They should share in personal evangelism. They should bring people to church. They should preach evangelistic messages, and no matter what it is they are preaching they should ask their listeners to repent and believe in Jesus.

However, one of the most important responsibilities of a pastor is to train the people to do the work of the ministry so the church is built up. This will require a planned and coordinated ministry effort to mobilize the people to evangelize. This does not mean that an evangelism program is all that is required for a church. This is not true either. However, there must be an educational component that facilitates the development of active evangelists in the local church.

I believe laypeople are the most strategic and underused tool for the work of world evangelization. I hold this belief for several reasons. First, laypeople scatter to the four winds after church on Sunday. Pastors cannot possibly go all the places the people go. The people could take the message to others that would never have heard the gospel.

Second, the power of multiplication kicks in when laypeople get involved. If the pastor does the work of

Evangel-lies

evangelism alone, the church will always grow by addition. If the pastor partners with and mobilizes the church, the church will grow by multiplication. The power of multiplication can change our communities and bring life to our church.

Third, I believe Jesus' command to "Go into the world…and make disciples" is a command every individual believer is to obey. This is a clear call for every member to evangelize.

I am not sure where I first heard the illustration, but it stuck with me. Think of the battlefield scenario. When an army takes to the battlefield who is it that goes into the trenches and fights the war? Is it the generals? No, it is the enlisted men. The generals give the commands, adjust the strategy, train the soldiers, and keep the supplies coming. It is the foot soldiers that win the war. The Bible teaches us that, as Christians, we are at war with Satan and the forces of evil. Pastors must model the behavior and preach the gospel, but they must also train the people and send them out to serve.

The challenge is daunting. Recent statistics tell us that 95 percent of American Christians never tell another person about Jesus. This is in their entire life. Maybe more troubling is the fact that most Christians do not view evangelism as their responsibility. America is fast becoming a secular nation. Some statistics tell us that only 4 percent of the millennial kids (those born within five years of the millennium) will remain in the evangelical church. When will America wake up and realize the world is coming to

Evangel-lies

Christ while America is dying as a Christian nation? Evangelism is every Christian's responsibility.

Lie #5: I would evangelize, but I can't go to visitation.

I hear this excuse all the time. I can't meet on Sunday afternoon or Monday night to take advantage of previously arranged evangelistic opportunities. Anyone have tickets to Monday night football? My point is made. We make time for what is important to us.

While program evangelism is not the most effective for reaching people for Christ, it may be the most effective in actually helping people get experience in sharing their faith. Program evangelism has many drawbacks, but the one thing it does have going for it is that it gets people out in the community talking about Jesus. The thing it doesn't have going for it is it can be impersonal and canned. This is a big challenge in the twenty-first century. We have lived in the fast food franchise century, but a new day has dawned. People are looking for personal interaction and authenticity. Visitation programs don't lend themselves to this kind of personalization.

I recommend relationship evangelization as the most effective and Christ-like evangelism program. Just as the title implies, it is personal. There is a relationship. There is concern and care. Jesus took time for people, and so should we. Get away from the canned and programmed approach and make your interaction about the gospel natural as soon as you can.

Evangel-lies

Evangelism may be learned within the structure of a program. Evangelism, however, is certainly not confined to a program. This is the danger of program evangelism. Christians can begin to think of evangelism as something they do at a particular time and place, and fail to practice evangelism as a way of life.

Matthew 28:19 is our clarion call for living a lifestyle of evangelism. Matthew uses the word *go* in a very particular way to tell us "as we are going." For you Greek scholars, it is in the aorist, passive voice. This means Jesus was very explicit about us telling others about Jesus all the time as we go about our daily activities.

Lie #6: I would evangelize, but everyone I know is already saved.

Some people say, "All the people I know are Christians." I would say to spice up your life. Get outside your religious box. Jesus did. He was a friend of sinners. He ate with them and went to their parties. He visited their homes. You should have non-Christian friends. You should love them, serve them, and spend large amounts of time with them. Anyone have Jewish friends? Muslim friends? Friends that are atheist? Good. Reach out and live a little. You will discover that Jesus is the best and you have something great to offer others. Make evangelism natural and relational by doing three things.

First, take advantage of your natural relationships with people and tell them about Jesus. This means you cannot be too busy. You must take time.

Evangel-lies

You must interact. You must converse with other people. Our challenge is that we live in a world that is increasingly shutting out other people. Christian people should be doing exactly the opposite. We should be looking to engage people relationally.

Second, you must be willing to open your eyes. You must see people as they really are. You must understand what is going on in their lives. You must be able to talk to them in their own language. This means you must identify with them. You must get involved. This is more complex than just taking a couple of hours on Monday night to visit. This is a lifetime of investment in your world and other people.

Third, God wants to help you perform this relationship evangelism. If you are under the impression that God has really never given you the opportunity to tell another person about Jesus, I want you to do something for me. I want you to put this book down and pray this prayer: "God, cross my path with someone who needs to know You love him or her." Now get up and go to a public place like a mall or park or gym, and start talking. I want you converse with them the way you would your best friend about the most important and significant thing in your life—God!

I have met many people who call themselves Christians, but the evidence of their lives indicates otherwise. Jesus said, "Not everyone who says to me Lord, Lord…will enter the kingdom of heaven." Jesus teaches us in the Sermon on the Mount that we will know people by their fruits. While it is not our place to serve as a person's eternal judge, Jesus does indicate that the fruit of a person's life indicates whether on not they are really born again. One fruit every true believer should bear is the fruit of a faithful witness for Christ.

Conclusion

Let me close by stating that not everyone who says they have trusted in Jesus is really saved. Many people I know say that their son, daughter, mother, or father once made a profession of faith in Christ. Therefore, they believe they are going to heaven. But are they really saved? You may argue that they raised their hand, went forward, and got baptized, etc., and that means they really got saved. The reality is that not everyone who performed one of these religious actions got saved.

Jesus taught us in the parable of the soils about four kinds of soil: the good, the hard, the thorny, and the rocky. Each type of soil represented the kind of heart the seed of the gospel found when it was planted in the heart of the listener.

Some gospel seeds are stolen away by Satan. He steals the truth away, and it never has a chance to take root in a person's life. Some are choked out by the cares of the world. This seed falls among the thorns. As the thorns grow, the message is never really able to grow. It's overwhelmed by the cares and the worries of the world. Some seed falls on shallow ground. They wither under the pressures of daily life. When the sun begins to burn down, their faith withers and disappears. The seed never grows to maturity.

Evangel-lies

If we look at statistics, we could conclude that only 25 percent of those who make a profession of faith in Jesus are really saved. The reality is that many people who call themselves Christians are not really saved. But some seed falls on good ground and grows up and yields a harvest. A harvest of love, joy, peace, patience, goodness, kindness, mercy and self-control (Galatians 5:22-23). This kind of harvest evidences the fact that Jesus really has saved us. Are you bearing fruit?

God wants you to be certain of your salvation. Assurance of salvation is a big issue for God. It is such a big deal that He wrote the entire Bible to discuss it with you. False conversions are such a big deal to God that He put 1 John in the Bible. The thesis of 1 John is found in 5:13: "I write these things to you so that you may know that you are saved." What are those things He writes about so that you can know you are saved?

He writes first about our right beliefs. God wants us to have right doctrinal beliefs. He knows that believing just anything won't save you. You must believe the truth of what God has done for you in Christ. We must believe that Jesus died in our place to pay the price for our sins and rose again to assure us that God accepted His sacrifice for our sins.

He writes next about right behavior. He echoes Jesus' words here: there must be transformation in our life that gives evidence of our salvation. Think about it with me. If God enters into a person's life when they come to Christ, shouldn't there be some

Evangel-lies

kind of significant change? Absolutely. John says this provides a second evidence of a person's salvation.

The final evidence of a person's salvation is that they have brotherly love. Born again people love others. They love the church. They love other Christians. They love the unlovable. They love because God has loved them.

God says if you have right beliefs, right behavior, and the right brotherly love, then there is evidence you really do know Jesus. God takes our salvation seriously. He wants you to know you are saved. Is there any evidence that you're a Christian? There should be, the Bible says, if you're really saved.

Rebecca Manley Pippert left the confines of the Bible Belt and moved to Portland, Oregon. She saw something in her local church that she wrote about in her book *Out of the Salt Shaker and into the World*. In it, she describes the church's responsibility to evangelize a lost world. She closes the book with this moving story: She went to church one day and saw an unusually dressed man come into the sanctuary. Everyone knew who he was. He was a college student who never combed his hair, carried his surfboard around town, and never wore shoes. He had never been seen in anything but blue jeans or shorts with a T-shirt on.

This unassuming college student got saved and decided he was going to go to church. The closest church to the college campus was a nice upper-middle-class church where everyone dressed nicely. The college student walked into church one Sunday and started looking for a seat. He couldn't find a seat,

Evangel-lies

so he finally just sat down on the front row on the floor. One of the ushers saw him and came walking down the aisle towards him. Everybody started shaking their heads. They knew what was about to happen. They reasoned to themselves, "You know, he just doesn't understand these kids today. You can't really blame him. His generation is so far removed from this boy's culture."

When the usher got to the front of the church, he leaned down to where the boy was sitting. He painfully stooped all the way down on the floor and sat on the floor next to him. The Good Samaritan reached out to the Prodigal Son. That is what God wants you to do. God wants us to be the Good Samaritan and reach out to His Prodigal Son.

Discussion Questions:

1. Discuss how you can be God's spokesperson in the places where God has already put you.

2. Discuss how you think a unique style of evangelism might fit you best.

3. Discuss how God wants to use the relationships you already have with people to share Jesus with others.

4. Discuss how you have limited or compartmentalized your witnessing.

Activities:

1. Go to a public place and start a discussion with someone you do not know about spiritual things. Direct it to the five parts of the gospel presentation.

2. Next time you are at school, work, or a park, look around and consider who is around you that God may want you to share Jesus with.

Chapter 3. Ananias
Acts 9:1-19

God has always been a God who intervenes in people's lives. One of the great stories of God's intervention in Christian history is the story of Francis Thompson's conversion. Thompson is most famous for his poem "The Hound of Heaven."

After experiencing a loveless childhood, Thompson tried to find meaning in life through his career, wealth, and power. He lived and worked in London, jumping from career to career looking for something that would satisfy him. His search for meaning almost destroyed him. He was living on the streets of London when a Christian couple met him and began to share Christ with him. Thompson followed Jesus and wrote a poem about his experience. He described how he spent his life searching for something meaningful only to discover God was searching for him all along. Two portions of his poem go like this:

Evangel-lies

I fled Him, down the nights and down the days;
I fled Him, down the arches of the years;
I fled Him, down the maze of passage ways
Of my own mind; and in the mist of tears
I hid from Him, and under running laughter.

* * * * * * *

Up vistaed hopes I sped;
And shot, precipitated,
And down Titanic glooms of chasmed fears,
From those strong Feet that followed,
followed after.
But with unhurrying chase,
And unperturbèd pace,
Deliberate speed, majestic instancy,
They beat—and a Voice beat.

I can identify with Thompson's experience. I discovered that God was patiently pursuing me while I thought I was pursuing fame, pleasure, and riches. The more I fled, the more He pursued me. I found I could not outrun Him or hide from Him. He would not be denied.

The Bible teaches us God is a God of intervention. God intervenes in our lives in order to draw us to Him. God intervenes in our lives because He desires to restore the broken relationship between Him and people. Since Adam and Eve sinned in the garden there has been a loss of fellowship between God and man. God has made possible the reconciliation of man through the sacrifice of Jesus Christ.

Evangel-lies

He has been seeking to restore our relationship with Him. God does this because He loves us, and His activity in our world takes place in an effort to intervene and accomplish His work.

God has a long history of intervening. The Bible is full of stories that describe God's intervention in people's lives. God intervened in Abraham's life when He chose to bless him. God intervened in Joseph's life in order to provide for Israel through the drought and build them into a nation. God intervened in Moses' life to rescue him from the Nile, educate him in Pharaoh's palace, and bring him out of the wilderness in order to deliver Israel from Egypt. God intervened in Jeremiah's life by calling him to serve as a prophet to tell Israel to repent. God intervened in Isaiah's life while he was in the temple to give him a heavenly vision. God, in His grace, actively pursues people. It is a gradual pursuit. It is a gentle pursuit. It is a gracious pursuit.

The Bible is filled not only with people who tell their intervention story. The Bible is also filled with verses that describe the activity of God as He pursues people. Psalm 23 says, "Surely goodness and mercy will follow me all the days of my life." The words "follow me" in Hebrew carry the idea of pursuing a person. It is like the sheepdog on the heels of the flock, pursuing them and guiding them along a path. God is dogging the steps of every living person seeking to establish a relationship with them. People may be scurrying around searching for something, but while they are searching for something, God is seeking them out.

Jesus' three parables found in Luke 15 also describe God's pursuit of people. The parable of the lost coin describes a widow looking for something precious. It reminds us how precious people are to God. The parable of the lost sheep describes the priority God places on searching for the lost. The parable of the prodigal son describes the pursuing love of the father that seeks the lost son. Jesus described His own ministry as coming to "seek and save what was lost" (Luke 19:10).

When we think about evangelism, some Christians think about the activity they perform. Few think about God's activity. Many Christians perform evangelism as if a person's conversion is completely up to them. This is not only bad evangelism. It is bad theology.

Acts 9 reveals that two parties are involved in the work of evangelism: God and man. God intervenes in lost people's lives, and Christians are to identify with lost people. Saul's conversion story describes both of these parts, God's intervention and Ananias' identification. Let us look first at God's intervention in Saul's life.

God intervenes in Saul's life

Saul's conversion story is probably the most famous and perhaps one of the most dramatic conversion experiences recorded in the Bible. Even today we describe some conversion testimonies as a "Damascus Road experience." In Acts 9:1-9 we read the story of God's intervention in Saul's life:

Evangel-lies

Meanwhile, Saul was still breathing out murderous threats against the Lord's disciples. He went to the high priest and asked him for letters to the synagogues in Damascus, so that if he found any there who belonged to the Way, whether men or women, he might take them as prisoners to Jerusalem. As he neared Damascus on his journey, suddenly a light from heaven flashed around him. He fell to the ground and heard a voice say to him, "Saul, Saul, why do you persecute me?"
"Who are you, Lord?" Saul asked.

"I am Jesus, whom you are persecuting," he replied. "Now get up and go into the city, and you will be told what you must do."

The men traveling with Saul stood there speechless; they heard the sound but did not see anyone. Saul got up from the ground, but when he opened his eyes he could see nothing. So they led him by the hand into Damascus. For three days he was blind, and did not eat or drink anything.

Acts 9:1-9

Exclusivity

Acts 9:1 says, "Saul was still breathing out murderous threats against the Lord's disciples." Saul believed the Jewish sect had to be eliminated or else it would threaten Israel. In the second verse these disciples were described as belonging to "the

Way." This is certainly a derogatory label used by the Jewish leadership to discredit them based on the exclusivity of Christ. While Christians were seeking to show people the way to Christ, Jews were mocking this new sect by referring to them as "the Way."

The term originated because Jesus claimed to be the way, the truth, and the life (John 14:6). This label certainly indicates the mission's emphasis of the early church. The church believed Jesus was the way to God. They were known for the message they preached, and they preached that people needed to follow Jesus. The description is repeated in Acts 19:9 and 23, so it was evidently a description detractors gave to the early church.

Twenty-first-century Christians should take note of the adverse reaction non-Christians have to the exclusive claims of Christ. Christians and churches still face a great challenge because of Christianity's exclusive claims. In our day of tolerance and pluralism, making exclusive faith claims is considered the one intolerable position.

As you become more active in sharing your faith, you must remember the exclusive nature of following Christ. You must be aware of how many people will respond to these claims. You must also be prepared to answer the questions as to why Jesus demands our exclusive loyalty. The answer is, of course, that there is no other name given under heaven by which men must be saved. Jesus plus nothing else is the right equation for salvation.

Saul's Hatred

Three times in the story of Acts we read about Saul's hatred toward Jesus and His followers. First, he supervised the cloakroom during the stoning of Stephen. He gave his approval to the action and supervised the execution (Acts 7:58). Saul held some position within the Sanhedrin that gave him authority and status among the mob that stoned Stephen. While Saul did not cast the stones, He was in full support of stoning Stephen. He gave his approval to Stephen's death and began a campaign of violence to squelch the Jewish sect that had claimed Jesus Christ was the Messiah.

You cannot help but anticipate in Luke's narration of the story church's history the conversion of Saul. His name is planted early in the story with the anticipation of his conversion. This particular event must have left an indelible mark in Saul's memory that God would later use. Luke recorded it probably because Paul had shared with him in their travels that this was the moment he became aware of God's pursuit.

Second, Saul undertook the task of single-handedly destroying the church. The idea is conveyed through Saul's use of brutality and cruelty to try to destroy the church (Acts 8:3). The word *destroy* indicates that he intentionally inflected pain on those who followed Jesus. He wanted them to suffer. He wanted to hurt them. His anger was so deep that he desired to inflict pain on them. It is impossible to not see a comparison being made between the anger and persecution on Saul's behalf and the love and devotion on the disciples'. Saul was angry, hateful,

Evangel-lies

and violent. The disciples were loving, forgiving, and devout.

Third, Saul became the self-appointed inquisitor for the Jews as they opposed the followers of Jesus (Acts 9:2). Saul secured extradition papers from the high priest as he pursued Christians who fled the country. He arrested not just men, but women and even boys and girls. He threw believers in prison for professing their faith in Christ. He probably tortured many of them to surrender the names and locations of the church's leaders and other followers. Saul had a twisted ambition and a deadly zeal, but each time Saul progressed in his persecution, God was planting seeds of the gospel in his life and continuing His pursuit of him.

Getting Your Attention

After more than one hundred miles on the Damascus Road, God broke into Saul's life unexpectedly. Acts 9:3 says, "Suddenly a light from heaven flashed around him." God stopped Saul dead in his tracks. God knew how to get Saul's attention, and you can be absolutely sure He knows how to get yours. God knows what it takes to garner every person's attention, and He is willing to use it to intervene in people's lives.

I am often asked why bad things happen to good people. Why do people die? Why do people suffer? There are no easy answers to these questions. We can be confident that God is at work in the midst of people's hurt. I think God takes all the pain and suffering and uses it to gain our attention. He uses

Evangel-lies

the suffering we all face in a sinful world to challenge our thinking and belief system. He sees our lives from an eternal perspective, and He therefore looks at our suffering as an effort to save people and change people.

One of the most significant problems people face in life is their physical death. The Bible goes so far as to say death is man's final enemy. The Bible teaches that God, in His grace, allowed physical death to enter the world when Adam and Eve sinned (Genesis 3:21-24). God allowed death to enter the human experience to force people to come face-to-face with their spiritual needs. These needs include the desire to live forever, to have peace within, and to find purpose in life. Each of these categories of human experience is imbedded into our lives. This is done in order for us to ask ultimate questions that force us to give God some kind of attention and consider the claims He has made.

God arrested Saul's attention with a light from heaven and by speaking in an audible voice. The voice was the voice of Jesus, and it confronted Saul as he persecuted the church. Jesus said, "Saul, Saul, why do you persecute me?" Saul was so overwhelmed by the light and the voice that he fell to the ground asking, "Who are you, Lord?" (v. 5)

Typical or Atypical?

Let's pause to ask an important question: Does Saul's conversion represent the typical conversion experience or is it atypical? The answer is both. God's intervention in Saul's life was in some ways extraordinary, and in other ways it was ordinary.

Evangel-lies

It is extraordinary that Saul was confronted with a bright light and an audible voice. Saul was confronted in a manner similar to that of Jeremiah, Isaiah, and Ezekiel. In order to be converted it is not necessary to have this kind of dramatic confrontation. We do not need to hear a voice, see a light, and fall to the ground.

Saul's encounter with God was a call to become an apostle. The biblical requirement to be an apostle was to have an encounter and calling from the resurrected Lord. Saul's conversion, therefore, was both a conversion and a calling.

At the same time, God's intervention in Saul's life is a typical conversion experience. Conversion requires a person to repent and place their faith in Christ. This is commonly referred to as establishing a personal relationship with God through Christ. This requires a person to believe that Jesus died and rose again for their sins and to place their faith in Jesus. This is what God requires of everyone who becomes a Christian. The Bible calls this a new birth. This is why Jesus said to Nicodemus, "You must be born again" (John 3:7). The essential feature is that every person must have a personal experience with God though Jesus Christ in order to be saved. Saul's salvation was just like every other Christian person's in this way.

Let's be cautious at this point. We do live in a world that doubts or is at least skeptical about the supernatural. I have been around long enough to know that God cannot be limited by what we think or believe about Him. This is His world, and He can break in and accomplish what He wants in the way He wants. We should not limit supernatural involvement in supernatural ways when it comes to evangelism. People can still have a Damascus Road experience. It is not beyond the realm of possibility.

Repentance and Faith

Let me again elaborate on repentance and faith. Some modern and post-modern Christians argue that only faith is required for the salvation experience to be genuine. They might allude to Jesus' encounter with the sinful woman (John 8:1-11), with the lepers (Matthew 8:1-4), or with any one of many other texts to prove their point. When a careful study of Scripture is made, one can easily see Jesus spoke to those who already had a repentant attitude about faith. To those who did not have a broken heart over their sin, Jesus spoke to them about both repentance and faith. Saul's story describes how he demonstrated his repentance by fasting for three days while he awaited God's messenger, Ananias.

Both faith and repentance are required for a person to be saved. These represent both a positive and a negative side of the conversion experience. The negative side is repentance. Repentance signifies that a person understands that God is right. God is right about man's sinful condition. God is right to judge and condemn people for their sins. A person must repent by both expressing sorrow over failing God and turning away from a sinful way of living. This is the repentance side of a person's salvation.

Evangel-lies

The positive side of salvation is faith. This is what a person turns toward. They turn to Christ, trusting in Him for their salvation. They believe that Jesus died in their place as a sufficient and acceptable sacrifice for their sins. He rose again, confirming that God the Father accepted God the Son's sacrificial death. They, by faith, believe that Jesus will accept them into heaven when they die. They depend on Jesus for forgiveness and eternity. They demonstrate this faith by letting Jesus reign as Lord over their life.

We should take note that while Jesus broke into Saul's life suddenly on the Damascus Road, God was patiently and progressively intervening in Saul's life. Saul's conversion came in a moment, but Saul could look back and see how God had been working toward the moment of conversion for a long time.

I have learned that God is often at work in people's lives, but they are not aware of it until after they have come to know Jesus. After their own conversion they can look back and see the path God took them down in life to lead them to a point of decision. It reminds me of a survey I once read that indicated the average Christian hears the gospel seven times before they come to know Jesus. This should encourage every believer to share his or her faith. If this number is true, you will only pray with a person to receive Christ every seven times you share your faith. Therefore, you need to remember that you are probably one in a long line of people God is using in another person's life in order to bring them to Christ.

God's patience was demonstrated toward Paul as he heard Stephen's witness, interacted with the apos-

Evangel-lies

tles, and observed the activity of the early church. It is not inconceivable to think that Paul may have even met Jesus during one or more of the feasts in Jerusalem. Their eyes may have met. Paul may have heard the teaching of the Lord. Only eternity will reveal how God's patient and benevolent grace was extended to Paul, but this much can be said: God was patiently pursuing Saul, and He is patiently pursuing people we know today.

God's gradual pursuit led to a defining moment in Saul's life. What would he do? Saul had known about God, but he did not know God. Saul had studied theology, but he had never met the God he studied about. Saul knew categories of religion, but he did not know his creator. Saul, when he came face to face with Jesus, caught a glimpse of God's glory, and he was so overwhelmed with it that he lost his sight. Saul went from being a proud, zealous, self-confident, arrogant opponent of Jesus to someone who was now humble, captive, and ready to listen to the Lord.

The Transition

"Who are you, Lord?" Saul would call out. God knew how to get Saul in a position to ask the most important question in life. This question takes us back to Jesus' meeting with His disciples in Caesarea Philippi. Here Jesus is camping with His disciples and asks them, "Who do men say that I am?" This, of course, is a prelude to the most important question a person will ever have to answer: "Who do you say that I am?" This is the most important question

Evangel-lies

because how a person answers this question will determine where a person spends eternity.

I have often used this question to transition a conversation. One of the most difficult things to do in witnessing is to transition the conversation. It is easy to introduce yourself, talk about your interests, and converse about family. The transition of the conversation is difficult. Jesus taught us to use a transitional question. It is open-ended and provides people the opportunity to give you insight into their spiritual beliefs.

If a person tells you they believe Jesus is their Savior who died for their sins, it lets you know you are talking with a believer. You can share your testimony and life experience with a new brother or sister in Christ. If the person tells you they think Jesus is a good teacher or philosopher or a good man, you know the person is not a Christian.

There are a number of good questions you should be ready to ask as you think about telling others about Jesus. Let me list several of them for you.

1. Who do you think Jesus is?
2. What do you think it takes for a person to go to heaven?
3. If you were to stand before God and have Him ask, "Why should I let you into heaven?" what would you say?
4. Have you ever come to the place in your life where you have trusted in Jesus as your Savior?

Evangel-lies

There are of course many other questions you can ask. You can also ask these questions in more customized ways to be more specific, depending on how your conversation is going and what you might need to know about the person. But remember to ask questions. You will learn a great deal about the person's spiritual condition when you ask questions and listen.

When Saul asks, "Who are you, Lord?" Jesus replies, "I am Jesus whom you are persecuting." The word *persecuting* literally means "whipping." Saul's persecution was against Jesus, even though Saul was punishing Jesus' followers. This helps me remember that every time I am persecuted, Jesus is feeling my pain. He empathizes with me and identifies with me in my suffering.

Verse 6 says, "Go into the city and you will be told what you must do." Notice that Saul's conversion is not on his terms, but on God's terms. It's God's plan of salvation, not man's plan of salvation. God negotiates with no man when it comes to the work of salvation. He has done what is necessary for a person to be saved.

I have met plenty of people who believe they have struck an agreement with God about what it takes for them to be accepted by Him. I can assure you that God makes no bargains with people other than the eternal transaction He initiated when Jesus Christ paid the price for our sins. No matter what a person says about coming to terms with God, if it is not based on Jesus it is not a legitimate deal.

Evangel-lies

The men traveling with Saul stood there speechless; they heard the sound but did not see anyone. Saul got up from the ground, but when he opened his eyes he could see nothing. So they led him by the hand into Damascus. For three days he was blind, and did not eat or drink anything.

Acts 9:7-9

The men who were with Saul were speechless. They heard the sound but did not see anyone. This still happens today. God can be speaking, and some people will hear and see Him while others cannot hear or see anything. One person who is in the Word of God hears and believes, while another person hears but never even begins to understand.

The same thing happens in churches all around the world today. God's Word will be preached and some people will leave the service being blessed by hearing God speak to them. Others will say they got nothing out of the service. How can this be? It is because of their hard hearts, blind eyes, and deaf ears. This says more about the person listening than it does the speaker. The Word of God will not return void, but often hard hearts prevent people from receiving God's Word.

There is obviously an object lesson within this story. Saul goes blind. It reveals to us his true condition. He was spiritually blind. The scholar could not see the truth. God used Saul's physical blindness to teach him about his spiritual blindness. God says,

Evangel-lies

"You're physically blind but can't you see you're also spiritually blind."

Saul went to Damascus to bind the hands of Christians and lead them away to prison. God intervened, and it ended up being Saul who was led away by the hand. What irony! Chapter 2 of Ephesians describes the life of a person who does not know the Lord. They're spiritually dead (v. 1); they follow the way of the world (v. 2); they're separated from God (v. 12); they're living without hope (v. 12); they are far away (v. 13). This is the pitiable condition of the person who does not know Christ.

God wants to change this. That is why He sent His Son into the world to live and die and rise again. God wants to change our condition, and that is why He intervenes in people's lives. God wants people to be saved by reestablishing a relationship with Him.

After meeting Jesus, verse 9 says Saul "did not eat or drink anything" for three days. He prayed. He fasted. Saul had some real soul-searching to do. He had to reevaluate everything he believed about his life. I think he prayed like never before. God had his attention.

God Is Still Intervening

God is still intervening in people's lives in order to establish a personal relationship with them. Before we consider how God uses ordinary Christians to get involved with people in the conversion process, let me present four ways God intervenes in a person's life to bring them to Christ.

Evangel-lies

First, God intervenes in a person's mind. God intervened in Saul's mind, and God is intervening in people's minds today. Saul was an educated man. He was educated under perhaps the most celebrated scholar of his day, Gamaliel. Gamaliel was aware of the prophecies of the Old Testament. Saul and his teacher certainly were among those anticipating the coming Messiah. They would have discussed these things regularly in the Sanhedrin. Saul read the law. He knew the prophecies. He observed Jesus' life. He was conscious of the coming Messiah. He was anticipating the coming Messiah. He even knew that the story of Jesus mirrored much of what the Messiah's coming would be like; and, as he would later reflect upon it, he would realize all the things he already knew about the Messiah were fulfilled in Jesus.

Can you imagine how Saul looked back on all the places in which God was intervening in his life? He could not recognize it at the time, but God was nonetheless at work in his life.

If Saul did observe Jesus in Jerusalem during one of the feasts, you can imagine that he listened in on His insightful teaching. Do you think he observed Jesus' gentleness? Do you think he was amazed by Jesus' miracles? Do you believe he was in awe of Jesus' authority? Can you imagine what he thought about His humility and meekness? Do you think he contrasted the love and dignity Jesus demonstrated toward people with the way the Pharisees treated people? What must Saul have thought about during those three days and nights he was blind?

Evangel-lies

God is still intervening in people's minds today. God is intervening in people's lives in the exact same way He intervened in Saul's mind. God has been and is still planting ideas and thoughts about Himself in people's lives. He is telling them they are created by Him. They are designed to live forever. He makes them consider why they are here. God's Spirit whispers in their ear that they are not a mistake. He gave them a conscience that tells them when something is right or wrong, good or bad. It is a part of God's divine image that is marred by sin, yet it is still in many ways intact. The Holy Spirit also convinces them that there is more than just what is seen. God is working to convince them that there is a God, and His world reveals what He is like. God was active in Saul's mind, and God is active in the minds of people today.

Second, God intervenes in a person's memory. Saul was present when Stephen was stoned. Saul observed how Stephen lived, spoke, and acted when challenged about his belief in Jesus. Stephen made the history of the Bible come alive by relating Jesus to what God had been doing throughout Israel's history. Saul watched Stephen face down a serious challenge with grace and dignity. Stephen died while forgiving those who took his life. This experience was etched in Saul's mind. There is no telling how many times that film rolled back through Saul's mind, when he was lying in his tent at night the week he was traveling to Damascus.

Let me speculate for one moment about what is not in Scripture. We know Saul was persecuting the

Evangel-lies

church. He had thrown many Christians in prison. He was trying to destroy the church. What we are not told is what Saul was hearing and seeing as he maliciously captured and tortured these Christians. I wonder how many of them witnessed to him. I wonder how many prayed for him. I wonder how many sang songs of praise like Paul himself would do with Silas in the prison cell. We don't know how it happened, but I am sure it happened. I said earlier that it usually takes hearing the story of Jesus seven times before a person is ready to respond to Christ. Saul did not respond the first time, but God continued to intervene.

Remember, every time you respond like Christ, every time you speak like Christ, every time you do a kind deed, every time you have a right attitude, or every time you speak a word aptly spoken, the Bible says those memories become planted in the mind of someone else. God will use these memories to draw them to Jesus. How many memories are you planting in the minds of unbelievers that reveal Christ to them?

Third, God intervenes in a person's conscience. Saul was a righteous man. As a matter of fact, he claimed in Romans 7 that he had never outwardly broken the law. Yet he had to confess that inwardly he was a sinner. It was the last commandment that challenged Saul. The tenth commandment says, "You shall not covet." Saul knew that in his own heart he had the lust of ambition and many other evil thoughts. He had evil desires in his heart that revealed his sin and guilt.

Evangel-lies

Today many people try to ignore their conscience. They dismiss what their mind tells them. The conscience is a gift from God. It is a part of what makes humans in the image of God. It is a part of what makes us unique. Many people, however, do not want to listen to their conscience. They dismiss it. The result is that they end up feeling guilty and seeing a psychologist or taking medication. Have you heard the term "carrying baggage"? It is an admission that we have violated our conscience and acted in defiance against God.

Many people try various options in order to deal with their baggage. They try psychology. They deal with it sociologically by saying everyone is in the same condition they are in. They try therapy in order to feel like they can get rid of it. They try to numb themselves with alcohol, drugs, vacations, sex, or money. The reality is that the conscience is guilty because the human ideal is present. Our conscience tells us what we have done is wrong. We see our failures and our struggles and recognize our need for something better.

This something better is a restored and personal relationship with God through Christ. That is why God is intervening in the lives of people. He cares about us. He wants us to be healed in the heart, mind, and soul. He wants our lives to be different and better and eternal.

Fourth, God intervenes in a person's spirit. A person is not just a body or even a body and a mind. The Bible tells us that a person is made up of a body, mind, and soul. There is a spiritual component to

Evangel-lies

our lives. In twenty-first-century America we are observing a revival of the spiritual. People are spiritually hungry. They are longing for the eternal, the supernatural, and the meaningful. There is a spiritual search going on. This is God's intervention in people's spirits.

Saul was on this search himself. Saul knew about God, but he didn't know who that God was. He knew how to describe God. He would have described God as transcendent, omnipotent, powerful, and holy, but he didn't know who God was. He had no relationship with Him. The Bible tells us God created us in His own image in order for us to have a relationship with Him. Within that relationship we find joy and meaning and purpose and hope and a secure eternity. When this is missing, our spirit is empty. Saul may have been a spiritual man by definition, but he didn't know God. The Bible says that God can fill our hearts. God is the one who comes into our heart and changes our life and gives us that kind of peace by ending the estrangement and establishing a relationship.

In *Surprised by Joy*, C. S. Lewis writes, "God is the divine angler playing His fish. He's the cat cornering the mouse. He's the hound chasing the fox. He's the divine chess player maneuvering his opponent until he achieves a check mate." God is intervening in our lives to bring us to the place where we recognize our need for Him.

We can say with confidence that the Holy Spirit was actively working to bring Saul to Christ. The Spirit was convicting him of his sin. He was convincing him that Jesus was the Messiah. God

Evangel-lies

---

showed him why he needed to repent and confess Jesus as Lord and Savior.

The good news is today is still the day of salvation. The Holy Spirit is active performing this same ministry in people's lives today as he was in Saul's day. God's desire is for you to become a partner in ministry with Him. He wants you to tell someone you know about how God changed your life.

God is actively intervening in people's lives, but God expects Christians to get involved in order to partner with Him in His work. Make no mistake, evangelism is God's work, but God has chosen to use His followers to help share the message. The Bible says, "We are ambassadors for Christ. God is making His appeal through us" (2 Corinthians 5:20). Notice how God got a little known layman named Ananias involved.

Involved in People's Lives

> In Damascus there was a disciple named Ananias. The Lord called to him in a vision, "Ananias!"
> "Yes, Lord," he answered.
>
> The Lord told him, "Go to the house of Judas on Straight Street and ask for a man from Tarsus named Saul, for he is praying. In a vision he has seen a man named Ananias come and place his hands on him to restore his sight."

Evangel-lies

"Lord," Ananias answered, "I have heard many reports about this man and all the harm he has done to your saints in Jerusalem. And he has come here with authority from the chief priests to arrest all who call on your name."

But the Lord said to Ananias, "Go! This man is my chosen instrument to carry my name before the Gentiles and their kings and before the people of Israel. I will show him how much he must suffer for my name."

Then Ananias went to the house and entered it. Placing his hands on Saul, he said, "Brother Saul, the Lord—Jesus, who appeared to you on the road as you were coming here—has sent me so that you may see again and be filled with the Holy Spirit." Immediately, something like scales fell from Saul's eyes, and he could see again. He got up and was baptized, and after taking some food, he regained his strength.

Acts 9:10-19

One scene closes and another scene opens. In one scene Saul is praying, fasting, and thinking about Jesus' appearance. He is reevaluating every dimension of his life. In another scene, God spoke to a layman named Ananias. God spoke to Ananias through a vision, and Ananias knew exactly who was calling. He knew how to discern the voice of

Evangel-lies

the Lord. When God spoke to him, Ananias knew it was God.

God tells Ananias to go to Straight Street and restore Saul's sight. God said Saul was expecting Ananias to come and help him. Can you imagine Ananias' reaction? "Saul, Lord? I have heard many reports about the harm he has done to believers in Jerusalem. Are you sure, Lord? You want me to go where, Lord?" There is no doubt that this was a life-threatening situation. Ananias knew it. He reminded God, as if God did not know, that Saul was coming to Damascus not to be converted but to confront the Christians. Word of Saul's coming arrived before he did. Believers knew what to expect, and they were preparing for the worst.

God, in His grace, provides Ananias insight into His work. God reveals to Ananias that Saul will be His mouthpiece to the Gentiles. He will speak before kings (Acts 24:1, 26:32) and the Gentiles. God indicated that Saul would suffer much for the name of Jesus. With these few insights and an obedient spirit, Ananias took his life in his hands and went to Saul.

Did you know God wants you to be involved in the lives of other people even at the risk of your personal safety and reputation? I know that most people don't want to be involved in other's lives. They think of it as messy, difficult, and challenging. In the twenty-first century people live behind gated communities, put their names on the National Do Not Call Registry, and screen phone calls. We want to hold people at a distance and keep them outside of our lives.

Evangel-lies

Jesus teaches us something different. His words challenge our lifestyles today. Jesus says that if you love and serve Him, you will love and serve others. Jesus teaches us that if we are going to follow Him, we must get involved in other people's lives, no matter how difficult it may be.

Ananias was an ordinary follower of Jesus. He wasn't one of the apostles. He wasn't a pastor or prophet. He was a disciple (Acts 9:10). He was a layman. God said to him, "Go and ask for a man named Saul." God indicated He had already prepared the way for Ananias.

God spiritually prepares the way for believers to go and share Christ with others. God intervened and got Saul's attention. God prepared Saul to hear from Ananias. But what is so amazing is that even though God had done all of this, He chose to use His people in the process.

Saul had a tough exterior, but God made him very aware of his need. People are just like Paul today. They have needs. They have significant needs. In the midst of those significant needs God is at work, and He asks us to get involved in His work. Think about this. God wants to use you to get involved in other people's lives.

Ananias had his fears, and he spoke to God about them. He did not want to suffer persecution. He did not want to go to prison. Ananias wanted to obey God more than he wanted to live an easy life. I fear that most American Christians reverse their priorities. They want an easy life, and then they want to follow Christ. As we think about witnessing for Christ, we

Evangel-lies

should speak to God about our fears and use His words of encouragement to overcome all our fears.

When you boil evangelism down to its execution you deal with two issues: obedience and love. Obedience asks whom you are going to obey, God or self. The second issue is whom you love more, God or self. Evangelism is an obedience and love issue. Verse 15 says, "Go." Will you go?

If you are not going, you are not obeying. The Great Commission given by Jesus in Matthew 28:18-20 describes our going. As we are going, we should be telling. Since we are on the move more than ever, we should be telling more people than ever. One of the excuses I hear about evangelism is that people are too busy to devote the time needed. In fact, the busier we are, the more opportunity we have to tell. We are meeting more people and going to more events, therefore, we have more opportunity than ever before. The sad reality is that we are going more but telling less. This is a love and obedience issue.

I have trained many people to share their faith in Christ. Every person I've ever taught initially said they couldn't do it. I asked them to simply go with me and listen as I shared Jesus. The amazing thing is that they discovered telling someone about Jesus in a natural and honest way is easy. They would say, "Pastor, I didn't know it was so simple." Absolutely. It's so simple. It's so simple to go and tell the story. After their first experience, they always are ready to learn how to share Jesus with others.

Verse 17 says, "Ananias went to the house, and he entered it." He didn't just stand on the door-

Evangel-lies

step. He walked all the way into the house and got involved in Saul's life. He got involved in a man's blindness. He got involved in a man's covetousness. He got involved with someone who was persecuting the church. He went all the way.

Verse 18 says, Ananias entered the house, laid his hands on Saul, and scales fell from his eyes. Immediately, Saul got up and was baptized. He ended his fast, and I am sure he asked Ananias many questions. Ananias got to be a part of a person's new birth. He got to be involved in the conversion of the single most influential Christian who ever lived. He got to make a difference in a person's life and in all of human history.

I have often asked myself why God would go to the trouble of using people in the work of evangelism. The reality is that God wants us to know and work with Him. There are some spiritual lessons you will only learn when you get involved in the lives of other people and tell them about Jesus. One of my favorite verses in the Bible is Philemon 6. It says, "I pray that you may be active in sharing your faith, so that you will have a full understanding of every good thing we have in Christ." I am going to make a bold statement. Read it carefully. After your salvation experience, you will learn more about God by witnessing than any other single thing you will do.

Let me close our biblical study by telling you a personal story. Years ago, when I was a little boy, my father would take me to our family farm to work. Early in the morning he would get me out of bed and we would spend the whole day working on

Evangel-lies

the farm together. Some days were hot. Some days were cold. Some days it was raining and some days it would snow.

We would work on tractors, mend fences, care for cattle, trim trees, mow fields, and bale hay. We did all kinds of things during the day. We would work, eat, play, shoot our guns, ride horses, and do all sorts of other exciting things. I look back on those long days and all the work we did with mixed feelings. While other friends were playing, going to ballgames, and hanging out at home, I was working. But on the other hand, while I was working with my dad, I learned things about him that I never would have known otherwise. More importantly, I was getting to know my dad.

Did you know that when you go to work in the ministry of evangelism you are doing your Father's business? You are going to learn about Him. You are going to learn about His nature, His character, His heart, and how much He loves you. Yes, evangelism is hard work. It involves you learning something and extending yourself. But getting involved in people's lives will make you know that you are doing something greater and bigger than yourself. So how do you get involved in people's lives? There are three things you must do: You identify with people, you identify God's work in their lives, and you identify their spiritual needs.

Identify with People

First, you identify with people. Identifying with people requires you to consider their life, feelings,

Evangel-lies

and experiences. Identifying with others requires you to love other people. The best ways to love others is to follow the New Testament example. A number of people have taught us how to execute the New Testament command to "love one another." Several reputable commentators have taught that a Christian is required to fulfill all the "one another" statements found in the Bible.

For instance, there are thirty-five one another commands in the New Testament. One of those is the command to love one another. The natural question is how do you love another person? The answer is best found in fulfilling the other thirty-four one another commandments. Let me make this clear. You can love another by caring for them, comforting them, encouraging them, serving them, being kind to them, etc. When we do these, we are fulfilling God's command to love one another.

Identifying with others like this takes time. It cannot be rushed. It means thinking about other people's conditions and situations and demonstrating thoughtfulness in what you say and do for them. This will require you to spend your time on other people and not just yourself. We must confess that we are very selfish people, especially when it comes to our time. If we are going to be good followers of Christ, we must be willing to go out of our way to involve ourselves in other people's lives.

Identifying with others is what Jesus did with us. He went out of His way to enter into Samaria and meet with the woman at the well (John 4). He passed by the tree where Zacchaeus was watching (Luke 19:1).

Evangel-lies

He stopped to spend time with the woman who had been bleeding for twelve years (Luke 8:45). Again and again, Jesus stopped and took time to identify with people. Ultimately, this is what chapter one of John's gospel describes Jesus as doing for mankind when He left heaven and came to earth. Jesus identified with mankind's condition and came and lived among us. Can we do any less than what Jesus did? Should we not follow the example of our Savior and identify with people?

Let me challenge the way you may be thinking about evangelism. Make sure you don't think about evangelism as a project. Instead, I want you to think about evangelism as people. You see, God loves people, not projects. It is so easy to make this mistake. I know many spouses who have made their husband or wife their evangelism project. In the end, they have done more harm than good. They end up pushing them further away from the Lord because their efforts have been loveless efforts. When evangelism is a project, our evangelism seems aloof, detached, and insincere.

Jesus' example of evangelism should be our model. The individual mattered to Jesus. Remember the woman at the well? Jesus left the comfort zone of His own people, Israel. He engaged not just a woman, but a Samaritan woman. She was an outcast of society. He got involved in the messy details of her life. He got His hands dirty with her problems. He transitioned from the earthly and religious matters to eternal and spiritual matters. He used a teaching tool, the water in the well, to help the woman identify with what He was saying. He took her physical need and showed her how it was a spiritual need. He helped her discover why she felt dirty and separated from God. He showed her how her bad sexual decisions made her sinful. He talked about how He could make her whole through faith and forgiveness.

Jesus identified with people, and if we are going to tell the story of salvation, we need to be people who identify with others. Who is it God has put in your path? How does He want you to identify with them? It's not your responsibility to save them. That's God's work. Your responsibility is to identify with them and then share Jesus with them.

Identify God's Work

Second, you need to identify how God is working in the lives of lost people. People who are not believers don't have the mind of God. They can't think spiritual thoughts. They're in darkness. They are like Saul. They have scales on their eyes. Saul knew many things, including things about God, but he could not see that Jesus was the Messiah. He needed Ananias to shine the light of God's truth into his life by pointing out what God was doing.

People who are living in darkness don't understand spiritual truths. Even the simplest things to a new believer are completely foreign to a person who does not know Christ. Understanding spiritual truth is like trying to understand a foreign language. When you have never been exposed to them, you can't understand them. You have no point of reference for them.

Evangel-lies

The Bible says Christians can know the thoughts of God. We can have the mind of God. This is a precious gift for believers, but believers must not forget that unbelievers do not have this ability. Believers, therefore, need to remember what it is like to be lost and help unbelievers identify God's work in their lives.

Let me tell a funny story that will help you understand why believers must tell unbelievers about how God is working in their lives. At the church I pastor, we translate our worship service into Spanish. While I am preaching, there is a translator in a booth who translates everything I say.

One day while I was preaching I started talking extemporaneously. Somehow I used the illustrative phrase "an albatross around your neck." It wasn't something that I put in my message notes that I had shared with my translator prior to the service. I later heard that my translator sat in the booth saying "Como se dice (How do you say?)? Ahh…umm…a dead pelican around your head." Understanding was lost in translation.

God wants you to be the interpreter for the lost people around you. You are God's translator to identify where and how God is working. You are the interpreter for the spiritual things that God is doing. This is how you identify God's work in a nonbeliever's life.

Identify the Spiritual Need

Finally, you need to identify spiritual needs. Everyone has spiritual needs. They may just not know

Evangel-lies

they exist because they can't identify or understand them. Again, they are not ignorant people. They are simply blind to this part of their life. These spiritual needs can most easily be identified as ultimate questions. People are already asking what have commonly been referred to as ultimate questions. These are life's big questions. Everyone asks these kinds of questions in some form or another. Let me address four of the most common ultimate questions.

First, people are asking questions like "Who am I?" What they are really asking is, "Do I have a unique identity, and does it matter whether or not I exist? This is a question of identity.

A lost person will answer their question about identity like this. They believe their life is the most important thing, so they build their life around themselves. They do what makes them happy. They accomplish everything they can. They try to gain the approval of others, all in an effort to discover who they are.

At some point they are going to doubt whether their life really matters. They are going to face questions about happiness and satisfaction and discover that they have nothing of ultimate value in which to believe. In the end, they will find themselves in one of two places. They will either end up with low self-esteem and occasionally be embarrassed by their life's happenings, or they will really succeed and become arrogant and proud of all they have accomplished. Yet they will wake up one day and realize their life is a sham. They will realize their life is empty and they will wonder why it happened and where they went wrong.

Evangel-lies

Unless there's somebody there to identify the spiritual need in their life and tell them how God can meet it, they're going be confused about their life. And, of course, God meets that need by saying, "Life's about serving Me, not about serving yourself." He wants them to find His love so that they can love and be loved unconditionally in their relationships with others.

Second, people are asking questions like "Why am I here?" What they are asking is a question about fulfillment. So what they do is design their own purposes for themselves, but it ends up not being satisfying or fulfilling. So they begin to pursue something else. They try to achieve something for themselves, but they end up feeling bored or frustrated or apathetic.

In this situation Christians need to interpret those spiritual needs by identifying them and helping them understand that God has a will for their life. Describing God's unique plan for their life can be one of the most powerful spiritual insights ever. This sense of fulfillment is powerful because everyone desires to do something meaningful with their life. Testifying about your own satisfaction and about how another person can find satisfaction is powerful.

Third, people are asking, "Why can't I get what I want?" People look to control their life by obtaining possessions. Possessions seem to provide security and satisfaction. Yet, when people do accumulate possessions, they end up being worried and burdened by what they have obtained. They are insecure and afraid someone might take it away from them. They are afraid they will lose what they have.

Evangel-lies

God wants you to identify with these kinds of people and show them that He is our only true security. What we have in this life is given to us by God to manage faithfully. We are to yield ownership to God and become stewards of what He has given us.

Finally, people are asking, "Why are my relationships not satisfying?" Worldly people are accustomed to using people, yet they are frustrated by the lack of significance in their friendships, marriages, and family. They become selfish in their relationships by trying to find people who will meet their needs. They end up lonely, alienated, and isolated. They are manipulative, insensitive, hostile, and critical.

God wants you to identify with them and demonstrate unconditional love by putting your love into action. You can show them authentic love by interacting with them in healthy ways. You can show them attention and Christian love. You can meet a need. You can be honest with them and speak the truth about life, love, and friendship. God wants you to be the bright light in someone else's dark world. He wants you to be involved while He is intervening. He has chosen to allow you to identify with them so that you not only learn something about someone else, but also about Him.

Let me close with a final story. Early one Sunday morning on May 26, 2002, a barge was going under a bridge along Interstate 40. The barge driver missed the gap between the bridge. The front of the barge caught one of the pillars and collapsed a six-hundred-foot section of the bridge crossing the Arkansas

Evangel-lies

River. Eleven people immediately died when the road collapsed into the river.

Fishermen in a bass fishing competition heard the crash and raced to the sight. One fisherman grabbed a flare out of his first aid kit and shot it up across the road. It struck the window of an eighteen-wheeler, whose driver immediately hit his brakes. His rig jack-knifed down the road and blocked all four lanes of the highway crossing that bridge. When the police arrived on the scene, the fisherman had made his way up to see how he could help. One of the police officers on the scene taking the report said, "Sir, what was it that you did?"

He replied, "I shot the flare."

God wants you to shoot the flare. You are the light God will use. Jesus said, "You will be fishers of men." God is intervening, and He wants you to get involved in His work.

The story of Saul's conversion highlights three more lies that prevent people from sharing their faith in Jesus with others. I have heard each one of these lies but have discovered that none of them are true. Fear can be overcome, opportunities abound, and God can change people's lives. Consider first the most common lie about evangelism.

Lie #7: I would evangelize, but I am too afraid.

I read a list of people's greatest fears not long ago. Number one on the list was public speaking. Number two? Dying! I thought about that for a minute and realized what it meant. At a funeral the person eulogizing the dead person is less comfortable than the

Evangel-lies

one in the coffin! Ironic, isn't it? Opening your mouth in a crowd or even opening your mouth to a single person to talk about your faith strikes fear in most people's hearts. I personally believe if a person can change the way they think about evangelism, it will alleviate their fear.

Ananias' fear of Saul was a reasonable fear. It was well-founded. He had reason to be afraid. Saul had a reputation for being ruthless with people, especially Christians. I can only imagine the thoughts and emotions that ran through his mind as he considered what God was asking him to do.

Ananias should be among the most commended Christians in the New Testament because of his quick and courageous obedience. The conversation went like this: God said to go. Ananias said he heard bad things. God said to go, Saul would have his own suffering. Then Ananias went. He placed his life in God's hands, and he went. Ananias loved God more than he feared Saul. This is the first mindset change that must take place. When your love for God trumps everything else, you will obey God instead of give in to fears.

Do you love God more then you fear others? I find that many Christian people live out of fear rather than love. The greatest verse in the Bible is "God so loves the world He gave His only Son that whoever believes in Him will not perish, but will have everlasting life" (John 3:16). The Great Commandment tells us to, "Love the Lord your God will all your heart and with all your soul and with all your mind" (Matthew 22:37). Paul describes in 1 Corinthians

13:13, "These three remain: faith, hope and love. But the greatest of these is love." The point I am making is that we should be living out of love, not out of fear. Yet when it comes to evangelism, far too many Christians are living out of fear.

Second, Christians need to speak up instead of remain silent. There is a new attitude in America about Christianity. Spirituality is being embraced, but Christianity is being shunned. Everything Christian is despised, but every other religion is accepted. As this has taken place, many Christians have silently sat on the sidelines and acquiesced to society's wishes.

This also happened in the New Testament. Look at Peter, for example. When confronted by a little girl in a public setting where Jesus was being tried, he was seized with fear after being asked a question. He stood near Jesus, and only hours after professing the thought that everyone else might desert Him, Peter declared he would never desert Jesus. Yet fear gripped his heart, and he denied ever knowing Jesus. Many of us are doing the same thing with our silence. We are denying Jesus. It is not necessary for Christians to speak boisterously or arrogantly. What is needed is a consistent Christian witness.

Every Christian should live as a good example of the Christian faith. They should faithfully tell the story of how Jesus has changed their life, and describe how God can change other's lives. Then they should leave the results to God by believing that He can take our witness and do something with it.

Third, Christians should remember salvation is God's work. It is not man's work. There is nothing

Evangel-lies

I can to do save a person. All I can do is join God in the work He commands me to do. This understanding should cause us to redefine success when it comes to evangelism. Success is not winning a lost person to Christ. Success is faithfully sharing Jesus in the power of the Holy Spirit and leaving the results to God. This definition of success alone can radically alter the way we think about evangelism.

Finally, Christians need to have greater confidence in God. He sent us. John 20:21 says, "As the Father has sent me, I am sending you." He has empowered us. Acts 1:8 says, "But you will receive power when the Holy Spirit comes upon you; and you will be my witnesses." He commands us. Matthew 28:19, echoing Jesus' final command, says, "Therefore go and make disciples." God is going to complete the work He is doing. We need to have confidence that God knows what He is doing, and we need to remain faithful to Him.

You don't need to worry about not knowing all the answers, being asked a question you don't know the answer to, failure, rejection, or any other fear you may have. Trust in the Lord with all your heart as you lovingly present Jesus to others. Remember Paul's words to Timothy in 2 Timothy 1:7: "God does not give us a spirit of fear, but of power of love and of a sound mind." Put this book down right now and ask God to change the way you think about evangelism.

Evangel-lies

Lie #8: I would evangelize, but God has never given me the opportunity.

John 4:35 is one of the most powerful verses for those considering evangelism. Jesus says, "Do you not say, 'There are still four months and then comes the harvest'? Behold, I say to you, lift up your eyes and look at the fields, for they are already white for harvest!" The disciples heard this admonition after returning with lunch only to find Jesus witnessing to the woman by the well. There is no telling how many people the disciples passed by going in and out of the city that day. But Jesus took advantage of the opportunity He had with a Samaritan woman.

It is like that in evangelism. We are passing opportunities every day without realizing it. We are waiting for an opportunity in the future only to pass by the harvest that awaits us now. Jesus tells us there are people everywhere looking, longing, and lingering. They are waiting for believers to tell them what they know about Jesus. The fields are bursting with opportunity.

Put yourself in a place of opportunity. Go to work, the park, your child's school, the mall, a sporting event, the beach, a coffeehouse, a restaurant, etc. The list is endless. Everywhere you go, there are people. People are lonely and spiritually hungry. They want to talk and share and interact. All you have to do is start the conversation, knowing you are going to go only as far as they will allow you to go in a conversation about God.

Not only are there so many places you can go to witness, there are so many ways you can witness.

Evangel-lies

You can converse. You can write a letter. You can make a phone call. You can send an email. You can invite them to church. You can take them to a special Christian event, like a concert or outreach. You can take them to a coffeehouse. You can go on a trip with them. You can play golf. You can participate in an activity or make a hospital visit. There are no limits on your opportunities. There are only excuses. Don't make excuses. Tell someone you know the story of God.

Lie #9: I would evangelize, but I don't believe God can change a person's life.

Is there anyone who is too far from God that they cannot be reached? The Bible tells us there is only one unpardonable sin: "blaspheming the Holy Spirit" (Matthew 12:31). Blaspheming against the Holy Spirit means that you are aware the Holy Spirit is at work and you still call it the work of Satan. This is the only unpardonable sin. Every other sin can be forgiven. This means that God is able to reach even the coldest and hardest of hearts. There are very few people that are outside the reach of God. Unfortunately, many Christians don't have faith that God is able to reach sinners. But, Jesus tells us He came to heal the sick, not those who are well. We should not be surprised that He does His best work saving and transforming those really far from Him.

Jesus demonstrated His ability to reach people while on earth by reaching the woman at the well, Matthew the tax collector, the woman caught in adul-

Evangel-lies

tery, the outcast lepers, and even the apostle Paul, who later considered himself the worst of sinners.

This is why Christians should not be surprised by deathbed and prison cell conversions. We should expect practicing homosexuals and pedophiles to be saved and changed. We can see prostitutes, drug addicts, and alcoholics be saved and changed. Hitmen, thieves, and perjurers can all be changed by the love of God. Prodigal sons can come home. There are people wallowing in all kinds of filth in all kinds of awful places, and they can come home. God can clean them up, put a ring on their finger, celebrate their homecoming, and elevate them to the position of a son. We should not be surprised at this. We should expect it.

Let's make this personal for a moment. Who is the person you know that seems to be furthest from the love of God? Is it an atheist? An adulterer? A homosexual? A murder? Do you believe God can reach them and change them? If you do believe He can, then you are demonstrating faith in God. You understand one of the most basic truths of Scripture. If you don't, then you just may be the older prodigal son yourself. You need to repent of your sin. You need to have faith in God and activate your trust by sharing your faith with those who seem to be furthest from God.

Discussion Questions:

1. How have you observed God getting someone's attention? How did He do it?

Evangel-lies

2. Discuss the five essential biblical truths a person needs to understand in order to be saved.

3. Discuss why it is so challenging to get involved in other people's lives and how you might do it better.

4. Discuss those fears that might prevent or deter you from sharing your faith in God with others.

5. Discuss how a person's perceived needs provide Christians the opportunity to tell how God can meet those needs.

Activities:

1. Make a list of your fears about evangelism, and beside each fear write how God wants you to adjust the way you think.

2. Make a list of people who are hostile toward God and begin to pray for their salvation and that God uses you to share Jesus with them.

Chapter 4. Cornelius
Acts 10:1-48

Years ago, D. L. Moody was scheduled to speak to Christians at an evangelism conference. Moody arrived early with his musician. The two stood on a street corner singing about Jesus in order to gather a crowd. After a crowd gathered, Moody stood up on a box outside the convention center and began preaching about Jesus. He preached the entire sermon without preparing a single thought. He simply preached the gospel to those who would listen.

Hundreds of people gave their life to Christ that day. As Moody began to close the sidewalk sermon, the convention attendees began to arrive. Moody closed the impromptu evangelistic meeting by saying, "I'm sorry no one else can be saved. The Christians now have to go and talk about evangelism."

Isn't this so true? We talk so much about evangelism and do so little. We talk about the story of Jesus, but we don't share the story of Jesus. We exhort ourselves to share Jesus, but we never execute evangelism.

Evangel-lies

In this chapter I want you to learn what God does to empower our evangelistic efforts. You will be surprised at how active God is. You will discover that you have a small but significant part to play. You are going to learn about God's preparation of the listener and the spokesman. You are going to understand that God has provided the message. Finally, you are going to learn that God produces the response.

While God is active in all of these ways, He asks you and me to get involved by sharing His story with others. We will close the chapter by understanding that God wants to use each of us in the lives of our friends and family to make sure they hear about salvation. God doesn't want us to buy the lie. He wants us to believe the truth.

The gospel is the only universal gift that has ever been offered. I am not saying that everyone is going to be saved. The belief that everyone is going to be saved is called Universalism. I am not talking about this. I am saying that there is no one excluded from the offer of salvation.

This was a strange idea for a first century Jew. They believed that God's offer of salvation was for Israel alone. Even Jesus' disciples limited their ministry to the Jews. It was a strange thought for them to consider allowing Samaritans and Gentiles into the church.

Since this is a long passage of Scripture, let me begin by pointing out the main theme found in verse 34: "Then Peter began to speak. I now realize that it is true that God does not show favoritism but accepts men from every nation who fear Him and who do what is right."

Peter comes to the place where he understands biblical prophecy. He no longer sees salvation as belonging only to the Jews. He understands that salvation comes to the entire world through the Jews. This salvation is offered to anyone who will repent and believe. Repentance and belief is what is required of anyone who will come to God through Christ. Salvation is universally available to anyone who will repent and believe.

The key question is has a person responded in faith and repentance? If they have, the Bible says that person's sins are forgiven and heaven awaits them when they die.

In our world today, we exclude people based on culture, race, education, social status, income level, and more. But the Bible says that God excludes no one and makes salvation available to everyone. Cornelius' story is divided into four parts. First, God prepares the listener. Second, God prepares the speaker. Third, God provides the message. Fourth, God produces the response.

God Prepares the Listener

> At Caesarea there was a man named Cornelius, a centurion in what was known as the Italian Regiment. He and all his family were devout and God-fearing; he gave generously to those in need and prayed to God regularly. One day at about three in the

Evangel-lies

---

afternoon he had a vision. He distinctly saw an angel of God, who came to him and said, "Cornelius!"

Cornelius stared at him in fear. "What is it, Lord?" he asked.

The angel answered, "Your prayers and gifts to the poor have come up as a memorial offering before God. Now send men to Joppa to bring back a man named Simon who is called Peter. He is staying with Simon the tanner, whose house is by the sea."

When the angel who spoke to him had gone, Cornelius called two of his servants and a devout soldier who was one of his attendants. He told them everything that had happened and sent them to Joppa.

Acts 10:1-8

First, God prepares the listener. Observe how God prepares Cornelius to hear the gospel. As you read the story, think about people you know whom God might be preparing to hear the gospel.

The story was set in Caesarea. Caesarea was a coastal town on the western border of Israel along the Mediterranean Sea. It was a prominent town. It was a wealthy town with a famous seaport. It was named for Julius Caesar. The Romans established Caesarea as their headquarters for that region of the world because of its easy access to Rome.

Evangel-lies

The Bible says that "there was a man named Cornelius" there. We know he was a Roman because he had a Roman name and a Roman job. He was a centurion in the decorated Italian Regiment. He was responsible for one hundred men, but he reported to his superior who was responsible for six hundred men. So Cornelius was, if you will, still in middle management. He was an ordinary guy going about his daily routine. But the Bible does make special mention of three unique things about Cornelius.

First, verse 2 tells us about his personal and spiritual life. Luke records that "He and all of his family were devout and God-fearing." This makes us aware that he was a family man. His family came with him from Italy. He didn't have to bring his family on this job, but he wanted his family to be together. Judea was considered a far outpost in an out-of-the-way place. But Cornelius knew it was important to pay whatever price he had to in order to keep the family together. This had a big payoff when he held his family conference in verse 33 and allowed Peter to witness to his whole family.

Second, verse 2 describes Cornelius as a devout and God-fearing man. Literally, Cornelius was moral and reverent. *Devout* means pious or godly, and *God-fearing* means being involved in religious activities. Cornelius recognized the spiritual dimension of his life. He thought being religious was important. He probably had many questions about why it was important, but for some reason he felt like it was important. There are a lot of people like Cornelius today. They are religious, but they are not right with

Evangel-lies

God, nor do they know what is required of them to be made right with God.

It is also important to take note of what the Bible does not say. The Bible does not say Cornelius was righteous. His men would later render their own personal opinion: "He is a righteous and god-fearing man" (Acts 10:22). Remember, man's opinion about being right with God rarely matches what the Bible says God requires. Righteousness means a person is right with God. The Bible says the only way to be righteous is to be made righteous by God. Romans 3:10 says, "There is no one righteous, not even one." Romans 3:21-22 describes how a person can be made righteous. The Bible says, "But now a righteousness from God, apart from law, has been made known, to which the Law and the Prophets testify. This righteousness from God comes through faith in Jesus Christ to all who believe." So Cornelius was religious, but he was not right with God.

Third, Luke also records that Cornelius "gave generously to those in need and prayed to God regularly." Cornelius was a man of religious conviction who demonstrated it through his personal and moral behavior. He financially assisted those in need. In other words, he not only had a conviction of heart, but he also lived out his conviction in his daily life.

The next verse says that he prayed at 3 p.m., which was the most important prayer time of the day. If you were religious, you certainly would pray at this time. Cornelius expressed his religious conviction through giving and praying.

Evangel-lies

The Bible doesn't say it, but Cornelius knew something was missing. There was more to life than his work, family, and religious activity. I personally believe the reason God allowed him to have his vision was because Cornelius was seeking after Him. Jeremiah 29:12-13 says, "Then you will call upon me and come and pray to me, and I will listen to you. You will seek me and find me when you seek me with all your heart." Cornelius was seeking God with all his heart, and God revealed Himself to him. Can't you imagine Cornelius experimenting with a variety of Jewish customs and rituals? Can't you see him talking to his family about how the paganism back in Rome compared and contrasted with the customs of Judaism? But what was he supposed to do? Where was he to gain insight?

God was about to break through into Cornelius' world. He would not argue about what God would say. God had been and was preparing him to hear the message of salvation. Cornelius' practice of religion brought him to the point of understanding he had a need for God.

Verse 3-4 says that while he was praying, he had a vision: "One day at about three in the afternoon he had a vision. He distinctly saw an angel of God, who came to him and said, 'Cornelius!' Cornelius stared at him in fear. 'What is it, Lord?' he asked." We are not told many details about the vision other than the fact that Cornelius saw a heavenly messenger. He was afraid, and he was about to receive the message from God through a man named Peter. The details were very specific. Peter could be found in Joppa,

Evangel-lies

and he was staying at Simeon the tanner's home. God had interrupted his life and prepared him to hear the gospel. The seed was ready to be sown. Just as Jesus described in the Parable of the Sower in Matthew 13:3-7, there was good soil for the seed. Peter was now ready to use his spiritual gift of evangelism with Cornelius. It is wonderful to observe how the details of Cornelius' story match the biblical pattern. Jesus told the Parable of the Talents in Matthew 25:14-30, and Peter would use his talent for evangelism to share Christ with Cornelius.

God is operating with a master plan, but we must remember it is His plan. Paul wrote about God's planning and purpose in 1 Corinthians 3:6-8: "I planted the seed, Apollos watered it, but God made it grow. So neither he who plants nor he who waters is anything, but only God, who makes things grow. The man who plants and the man who waters have one purpose, and each will be rewarded according to his own labor." Yes, Christians get to be a part of the work of evangelism, but only God can make the seed grow. Only God can bring a person to the place where they are ready to hear the gospel.

God Prepares the Spokesman

> About noon the following day as they were on their journey and approaching the city, Peter went up on the roof to pray. He became hungry and wanted something to eat, and while the meal was being prepared, he fell into a trance. He saw heaven opened and

Evangel-lies

something like a large sheet being let down to earth by its four corners. It contained all kinds of four-footed animals, as well as reptiles of the earth and birds of the air. Then a voice told him, "Get up, Peter. Kill and eat."

"Surely not, Lord!" Peter replied. "I have never eaten anything impure or unclean."

The voice spoke to him a second time, "Do not call anything impure that God has made clean."

This happened three times, and immediately the sheet was taken back to heaven.

While Peter was wondering about the meaning of the vision, the men sent by Cornelius found out where Simon's house was and stopped at the gate. [18] They called out, asking if Simon who was known as Peter was staying there.

While Peter was still thinking about the vision, the Spirit said to him, "Simon, three men are looking for you. So get up and go downstairs. Do not hesitate to go with them, for I have sent them."

Peter went down and said to the men, "I'm the one you're looking for. Why have you come?"

Evangel-lies

The men replied, "We have come from Cornelius the centurion. He is a righteous and God-fearing man, who is respected by all the Jewish people. A holy angel told him to have you come to his house so that he could hear what you have to say." Then Peter invited the men into the house to be his guests.

The next day Peter started out with them, and some of the brothers from Joppa went along. The following day he arrived in Caesarea. Cornelius was expecting them and had called together his relatives and close friends. As Peter entered the house, Cornelius met him and fell at his feet in reverence. But Peter made him get up. "Stand up," he said, "I am only a man myself."

Talking with him, Peter went inside and found a large gathering of people. He said to them: "You are well aware that it is against our law for a Jew to associate with a Gentile or visit him. But God has shown me that I should not call any man impure or unclean. So when I was sent for, I came without raising any objection. May I ask why you sent for me?"

Cornelius answered: "Four days ago I was in my house praying at this hour, at three in the afternoon. Suddenly a man in shining clothes stood before me and said, 'Cornelius, God has heard your prayer and remembered your

Evangel-lies

gifts to the poor. Send to Joppa for Simon who is called Peter. He is a guest in the home of Simon the tanner, who lives by the sea.' So I sent for you immediately, and it was good of you to come. Now we are all here in the presence of God to listen to everything the Lord has commanded you to tell us."

Acts 10:9-33

Second, God prepares the spokesman. As Cornelius's men approached the city, Peter began to pray. While praying, he became hungry. God used Peter's hunger as an object lesson. God wanted to show Peter what he was about to do. God wanted him to know it was all right to go to the Gentiles, so God showed him a vision. Verses 11-14 say, "He saw Heaven opened and something like a large sheet being let down to earth by its four corners. It contained all kinds of four-footed animals as well as reptiles of the earth and birds of the air. Then a voice told him, 'Get up, Peter. Kill and eat.' 'Surely not, LORD!' Peter replied. 'I have never eaten anything impure or unclean.'" Peter is referencing chapter 11 in Leviticus. God is asking him to eat the things that are on the list of strictly prohibited foods.

Peter must reason that God is testing him, and he does not want to fail. He failed Jesus many times, but this time he wanted to get it right. Yet he has this same vision three times. The repetition must have taken him back to when Jesus restored him after the resurrection. God says, "Peter, don't call impure what I have made pure." Peter must have had a diffi-

Evangel-lies

cult time understanding. This command was contradictory to everything he had ever learned. Peter was trying to understand what this vision meant when Cornelius' men knocked on the door. At that moment, God made Peter aware that three men were looking for him. So he got up and went downstairs to greet the men.

When Peter met the three men, he knew instantly what the vision meant. God was teaching him that people were not unclean. The three men recounted the story of how they ended up on Peter's doorstep. Peter made a significant gesture that no Jew would have considered making. Verse 23 indicates Peter invited them into the house where he was staying. This tells us Peter understood what God was teaching him through the vision.

There are some important points to make in this particular passage of Scripture. First, if you look in verse 23, you will realize they are going from Joppa to a Gentile city to tell of Jesus. No Jew could ever imagine that the Gentiles would be worthy of receiving the gospel. We cannot understand the barriers between Peter, a Jew, and Cornelius, a Gentile. But God intervened to prepare the spokesman.

If you remember the story of Jonah, you will remember Jonah was sent by God to Nineveh to preach repentance. It was in Joppa, however, that Jonah hopped a ship to flee from God. Interestingly enough, Peter was also in Joppa. Jonah fled from God, but Peter obeyed God. Jonah said, "God, not me! I don't want to go there. I can't be used in Nineveh. God, this is outside of my comfort zone. There's no

Evangel-lies

way I'm going." Peter saw the vision from the Lord and realized that God was doing something new.

Peter must have reflected upon what he saw in Samaria when the Samaritans came to Christ. He must have marveled that the godless Samaritans actually got saved. The disciples must have marveled that they actually repented of their sins and received the Holy Spirit. Peter must have thought about Jesus' words in John 14:12: "Most assuredly, I say to you, he who believes in Me, the works that I do he will do also; and greater works than these he will do, because I go to My Father."

There are many Christians who need the kind of radical preparation to do evangelism that Peter had. Many Christians need an epiphany before coming to evangelism. We make excuses and believe the lies, but when God boils it down for us, we're all in Joppa. The issue is whether or not we are going to flee from Joppa or follow God out of Joppa.

Peter had what I call a "significant emotional experience" that adjusted his life. I got that term from my dad. My dad supervised a large number of employees in a manufacturing company. When we were together, he would often tell me about his work. There were always challenging employees. Sometimes he would describe their situation.

He recounted how he had an employee who wasn't getting the job done. He couldn't see the bigger picture of what the company was doing. He would try to redirect them through reviews and evaluations, but some employees would not get it. I remember the first time I heard my dad said, "I am

Evangel-lies

going to give them a significant emotional experience." I knew what that meant. It meant my dad was going to say, "You are getting downsized, demoted, fired, or relocated." He knew there were certain pejorative words that would get their attention.

Do you know what we need when it comes to evangelism? We need a significant emotional experience. The reality is that people are not telling the story of God to lost people. The reality is that we don't take evangelism seriously.

I had a significant emotional experience related to my own personal evangelism that changed me. I was a new pastor with a small group of people in North Atlanta. A lady walked through the door of our church just a few weeks into my ministry. She was a sweet little old lady. She came into church crying. I spoke with her for a few minutes before church began and learned her husband was in the hospital and was very ill. I put my arm around her and prayed for her husband. I told her I would go visit him the next day.

The next morning I made the trip to Northside Hospital in Atlanta. I went to his room. I spoke with the man for a few minutes and prayed for him. The thought crossed my mind that I should share the story of Jesus with him, but I decided I did not have enough of a relationship with him, so I waited. I justified my delay by saying I would come back later in the week and share the Lord with him.

I did go back later in the week. I made my way to the room. It was empty. I asked the nurse where the man was, and she informed me he had died. I was shocked. The first thought I had was, "I wonder where he will spend eternity?" I walked down the hall of the hospital and ran into the nice lady. I put my arms around her. Through her sobs, I could hear her ask, "I wonder if he is in heaven or hell?"

This was my significant emotional experience. I was so distraught I committed to the Lord that I would never walk out of a hospital room without asking about a person's salvation. You need to have a significant emotional experience with evangelism. Churches need to have significant emotional experiences that change the way people think about evangelism. God prepares us to share the story of salvation with everyone no matter where they are from or what their condition is.

God Provides the Message

> Then Peter began to speak: "I now realize how true it is that God does not show favoritism but accepts men from every nation who fear him and do what is right. You know the message God sent to the people of Israel, telling the good news of peace through Jesus Christ, who is Lord of all. You know what has happened throughout Judea, beginning in Galilee after the baptism that John preached— [38] how God anointed Jesus of Nazareth with the Holy Spirit and power, and how he went around doing good and healing all who were under the power of the devil, because God was with him.

Evangel-lies

"We are witnesses of everything he did in the country of the Jews and in Jerusalem. They killed him by hanging him on a tree, but God raised him from the dead on the third day and caused him to be seen. He was not seen by all the people, but by witnesses whom God had already chosen—by us who ate and drank with him after he rose from the dead. He commanded us to preach to the people and to testify that he is the one whom God appointed as judge of the living and the dead. All the prophets testify about him that everyone who believes in him receives forgiveness of sins through his name."

Acts 10:34-43

Third, God provides the message for Peter to speak. Verse 24 tells us Peter arrived two days later in Caesarea. Cornelius was so excited that he gathered his family and friends together to hear him speak. Cornelius received Peter with reverence and dignity. Cornelius brought Peter before the large group gathered in his home. Peter spoke to them about his experience. First, he acknowledged it was strange to be in a Gentile's home (v. 28). Second, he acknowledged God did not show favoritism and accepted all kinds of people (v. 34). Third, Peter made the connection that the only people who were separated from God were those who rejected the reconciliation that God made for them through Jesus Christ (v. 39).

Look at verses 35 and 36. Here you will see again how simple the story of salvation is. The story goes

Evangel-lies

like this: in verse 37, Peter says Jesus lived among us and demonstrated who He was by His miracles and good deeds. In verse 39, Jesus was crucified on the cross. In verse 40, Jesus rose again because death had no control over Him. Notice again these three simple points. Jesus lived and had a ministry. Jesus died on the cross to pay the price for our sins. Jesus rose again, validating what God said He would do. This is the entire story. It is so clear and so simple. All we must do is share it.

Some people make excuses like "I never have a Bible or tract or resource to help me when I seem to need it." Let me give you one today. It is so simple. It is almost silly. It's your hand. First, take your hand and hold out your five fingers. Grab your thumb. It is a hitchhiker's sign for "give me a lift." Everybody needs a free ride with God. Everybody needs a ride to heaven.

Second, take your pointer finger. Put all the other ones down. The one finger reminds you that everyone has one problem sin. The Bible says, "All have sinned and fallen short of the glory of God."

Third, hold up all three of the fingers that are in the middle of your hand. Tell how there were three crosses on a hill one day, and Jesus was on the one in the center. There He shed His blood on the cross to pay the price for our sins.

Fourth, your ring finger represents commitment. What is required for your sin to be forgiven and for you to go to heaven? You must make a commitment to Christ. You must ask Him to forgive your sins and you must commit your life to Him.

Evangel-lies

Finally, look at your pinky. What does it take? It takes one small step of faith. The little finger represents the little bit of faith that will move a mountain.

This little reminder can help you always be ready to share your faith in Christ. It's so simple. God has provided you the message. Remember, God not only prepares the hearer and the spokesman, but God also provides the message.

God Produces the Response

> While Peter was still speaking these words, the Holy Spirit came on all who heard the message. The circumcised believers who had come with Peter were astonished that the gift of the Holy Spirit had been poured out even on the Gentiles. For they heard them speaking in tongues and praising God.
>
> Then Peter said, "Can anyone keep these people from being baptized with water? They have received the Holy Spirit just as we have." So he ordered that they be baptized in the name of Jesus Christ. Then they asked Peter to stay with them for a few days.
> Acts 10:44-48

Fourth, God produces the response. Verse 44 says, "While Peter was still speaking these words, the Holy Spirit came on all who heard the message." Peter's witness evoked the response of repentance

Evangel-lies

and faith. Cornelius, along with his family and friends, believed the message about Jesus.

Verse 45 says, "The circumcised believers (the Jews) who had come with Peter were astonished that the gift of the Holy Spirit had been poured out even on the Gentiles." The Jews couldn't believe what was happening. They considered Gentiles to be outsiders, but God had included them in the baptism of the Holy Spirit. They probably would not have believed it if they had not heard them speak in the same tongues they had earlier spoken with themselves.

Verse 46 indicates the Jews heard them "speaking in tongues and praising God" just like the Jews did on the day of Pentecost. Now all three groups of people—Jews, Samaritans, and Gentiles—had received the Holy Spirit. The gift of tongues had accomplished something wonderful. It gave evidence of God's forgiveness and acceptance to Jews, Samaritans, and Gentiles.

The Jews realized that God had not only reconciled people to Himself, but He had reconciled Jew and Gentile. They came to understand that the gospel was for everyone and that God could reach anyone.

Peter acknowledged that the Gentiles had been baptized by the Holy Spirit. He reasoned that if God had already baptized them with the Holy Spirit, there was no reason to "keep these people from being baptized with water." He baptized them all. Why did he baptize them? He baptized them as a public testimony of what God had privately and personally done with each of them.

Baptism

There has been a lack of emphasis on baptism in recent years. Let me add three comments about the baptism of new believers. First, baptism is not required for a person to be saved, but baptism is a believer's first act of obedience after they have trusted Jesus. Jesus commanded that we follow Him in believer's baptism. If Jesus went to such great lengths to be baptized by John the Baptist in the Jordan, then we should go to the same lengths to follow Him in His example.

Second, baptism is a symbol. It symbolizes that the candidate believes Jesus died and rose again for them. It likewise symbolizes that they have died to the consequences of their sin and are raised to live a new life in Christ. To best demonstrate this, baptism by immersion is required.

Third, baptism is a testimony. It tells everyone present that the person being baptized is identifying with Jesus. Baptism is exhibiting for others on the outside what a believer knows Jesus has done for them on the inside. This is the confession on earth that prompts Jesus' confession of His children to the Father in heaven.

Follow Up

Immediately after their salvation and baptism, verse 48 indicates that "they asked Peter to stay with them a few days." Peter was shoring up the essential elements in these new believer's lives. The most basic instruction would include four areas. First, there was a need for basic biblical and doctrinal instruction.

Evangel-lies

Every new believer in Christ is susceptible to wrong doctrine and bad theology. Peter was ensuring that the new believers had a good foundation in the truth.

Second, there was a need to emphasize corporate worship. It seems as though even prior to their salvation, a home church was being started. Cornelius had invited his family and friends to his home, where a large number of people gathered. It is not mentioned, but we can be fairly confident that their group did not stop meeting after Peter returned to Jerusalem. They would meet for preaching, praise, and prayer. All of these have been a part of Christian worship from the earliest days of the Christian church.

Third, there was a need for fellowship within this newly established community. Peter's remaining with Cornelius and his family certainly is a demonstration of solidarity with these new Gentile converts. The need for a continued community of Christian support did not end with Peter's departure. Every new believer needs a church community to love, support, and encourage them. This support often comes in the form of ministry and spiritual encouragement, but it certainly can take many other forms. What is important for new believers is that they continue to see the work of Jesus expressed through the love and ministry of the local church.

It is impossible to think of a Christian existing outside of a church. Imagining a Christian without a church is impossible. Many so-called Christians have left the church, saying it detracts from their faith. This is from the New Testament's point of view. Christ died for His church. He loves His church. The church has many failings because it is made up of imperfect people. The church is, however, the place where Christians live, love, and learn together.

Finally, there is a need to learn Christian service. The best place to learn to serve others is in the church. The Bible says when a person is saved, the Holy Spirit imparts spiritual gifts to them. These gifts are given in order to serve others within the church. The gifts are not intended to be selfishly used, but to sacrificially serve others in order to build up Christ's church.

Producing Results

Let me close our biblical study by addressing evangelism's results and God's sovereign work. It is important to remember that God is the One who works to produce all of these results. I know many churches and many denominations that believe their good works, hard works, and manipulated works can produce results. While there may be numerous results that are visible to the human eye, these are not spiritual results that are eternal.

Two scriptures are important to remember when thinking about results. First Corinthians 3:6-7 says, "I planted the seed, Apollos watered it, but God made it grow. So neither he who plants nor he who waters is anything, but only God, who makes things grow." Even with our best efforts, a person's salvation is not dependent upon any human being. We may participate by showing a good example, speaking a timely word, sharing our testimony, or telling the story of salvation. However, unless God is drawing a person, they will not come to Christ.

Evangel-lies

John 6:44 says, "No one can come to me unless the Father who sent me draws him." In verse 65, Jesus goes on to say, "No one can come to me unless the Father has enabled him." *Enabled* is the best word. It carries with it the idea of bringing a person into the presence of royalty. The reality is that there must be a person who makes it possible for them to come to the King. The person is, therefore, the enabler. God has enabled people to come to Him through Jesus.

God's participation and control over our evangelism efforts should not make us any less urgent, sincere, or dutiful when it comes to evangelism. God has chosen to involve us in His work of evangelism, and we are dependent on Him for the results. Our motive also should be right when we participate in evangelism. The only right motives are a love for God and a love for people.

Let me close by addressing three final lies: the lie of failure, the lie of offense, and the lie of human effort.

Lie #10: I would evangelize, but I might fail.

This is one of the biggest fears related to evangelism. We live in a success-driven world, time, and society. Many Christians have bought into a modern worldview which bases self-esteem on success. The reason many Christians have this fear of failing is because they do not understand what constitutes success. Success does not mean bringing someone to Christ every time you share Jesus. This is a mistaken concept of evangelism. Many think they are responsible for convicting, converting, and convincing a person to

Evangel-lies

come to Christ. Only the Holy Spirit can do these jobs. Remember, the average person hears the gospel seven times before they receive Christ. Therefore, we need a new definition of success for evangelism.

Perhaps the best definition I have heard was in my Campus Crusade Bible study in college. My leader said, "A successful witnessing experience is presenting the gospel in the power of the Holy Spirit and leaving the results to God." If Christians did this, there would be many more people sharing their faith with others. The only way you can fail at evangelism is to not do it, but the reality is that most people are failing by not sharing their faith.

Lie #11: I would evangelize, but I don't want to offend anyone.

This is a different kind of objection. The reason is that the Bible says the gospel is offensive to some people. Jeremiah 6:10 says it most explicitly: "The word of the LORD is offensive to them." The New Testament vividly describes how the gospel story of Jesus divides. 1 Peter 2:8 says the gospel is "a stone that causes men to stumble."

We should not be surprised that people stumble over the gospel. Paul referred to it as "the offense of the cross" (Galatians 5:11). Paul taught in 1 Corinthians 1 that the gospel was "a stumbling block to the Jews and foolishness to Gentiles" (1 Corinthians 1:23). He goes on to describe how it is the power and wisdom of God for those who believe.

Simeon prophesied that Jesus would divide and separate people in Luke 2. Simeon used three images

Evangel-lies

to describe how Jesus would divide believers from unbelievers. The images are the stone, the sign, and the sword. First, Simeon spoke about the stone. It was a stone in the path of life that either helped people step up into salvation or stumble and fall. The imagery was from the Old Testament (Genesis 49:24, Psalm 18:2, 71:3, Deuteronomy 32:31). There were also prophecies about the stone related to the coming Messiah (Psalm 118:22). The prophecy was that the nation of Israel would stumble over Him, but many would rise up to salvation at His coming. Both Peter and Paul used this image to describe their own ministries.

Second, Simeon spoke about the sign. Signs were special revealed truths that indicated Jesus was the Messiah. John outlined his gospel with the seven signs Jesus gave that proved He was the Messiah. John's signs included turning water into wine, healing the nobleman's son, healing the man at the pool of Bethesda, feeding the five thousand, walking on water, healing the man born blind, and the raising of Lazarus. Those who accept the signs receive eternal life. Those who reject the signs do not receive eternal life.

Third, Simeon spoke about the sword. The sword is none other than the sword of the Word of God that convicts people of their sin and judges their life. Hebrews 4:12 says, "For the word of God is living and active. Sharper than any double-edged sword, it penetrates even to dividing soul and spirit, joints and marrow; it judges the thoughts and attitudes of the heart." Those who let the Word of God divide their life come to Christ. Those who reject the Word of

Evangel-lies

God will one day stand before God, and His Word will judge them (Revelation 1:16).

The gospel is offensive, and there is no way around it. There is, however, an admonition for believers. While the gospel is offensive, our lives and our presentation of the gospel should not be offensive. The gospel is offensive because it tells people they are sinners. Our lives should have the opposite effect. People should be able to see the love of God in our lives, and that love should attract them to Jesus. The love Christians demonstrate toward them should help them climb upon the rock of their salvation.

The Bible repeatedly describes how wonderful and beautiful the love of God is. There is nothing in the world that is like the love of God. As the love of God shines through believers, people will see it is wonderful and beautiful.

Paul said in 2 Corinthians 4:4-10, "The god of this age has blinded the minds of unbelievers, so that they cannot see the light of the gospel of the glory of Christ, who is the image of God. For we do not preach ourselves, but Jesus Christ as Lord, and ourselves as your servants for Jesus' sake. For God, who said, 'Let light shine out of darkness,' made his light shine in our hearts to give us the light of the knowledge of the glory of God in the face of Christ. But we have this treasure in jars of clay to show that this all-surpassing power is from God and not from us. We are hard pressed on every side, but not crushed; perplexed, but not in despair; persecuted, but not abandoned; struck down, but not destroyed. We always carry around in our body the death of

Jesus, so that the life of Jesus may also be revealed in our body." The one thing that does help people over the stumbling block is the love of God and the love of His people.

Lie #12: If I don't evangelize, people won't get saved.

There are two sides to the work of evangelism. Man's side in the work of evangelism is to share the message that God loves rebellious people. Believers should communicate the gospel in a way that shares information and extends an invitation. The information is about what God has done through the person and work of Jesus Christ, and the invitation includes a summons to repent and believe.

The Christian is sent into the world to be Christ's ambassador and to share the message with as many people as possible. They share the message because of both love and obligation. Therefore, it is both a responsibility and a privilege for believers to share Jesus with others.

God also obligates Himself in the work of evangelism. God created mankind. He gave the law to convict people of sin. He sent His Son to be the Savior of the world. He offered His Son as a sacrifice on the cross. He raised His Son from the dead. He sent the Holy Spirit to convict people of their sins and convince them of their need for salvation through Him. He provided His Word to tell the story of Christ and instruct believers about how to follow Christ.

Can you see the partnership in the ministry of evangelism? Be careful, however. If believers want

Evangel-lies

to think of themselves as partners with God in the work of salvation, the believer is certainly the junior partner. God is the senior partner. The Bible tells us God controls human events. He calls to order the universe. He is sovereign in all things. While this may seem contradictory to the human perspective, it is not from God's perspective. He speaks of this in His Word. Psalm 33:11 says, "But the plans of the LORD stand firm forever, the purposes of his heart through all generations." The will and the work of God will never be thwarted. God is a loving, rescuing God who is working to save people. If believers do not partner with God in the work of evangelism, the very rocks will cry out.

Ephesians 1:4-5 says, "For he chose us in him before the creation of the world to be holy and blameless in his sight. In love he predestined us to be adopted as his sons through Jesus Christ, in accordance with his pleasure and will." Is that not the most amazing fact? God chose us. All along we thought we were choosing Him, but only after we are saved do we discover that God in fact chose us. Don't ever forget that God is a saving God, and He chose to let us participate in the work of evangelism. This is a high calling and privilege.

Evangel-lies

Discussion Questions:

1. Discuss how God has been preparing you to share the story of salvation.

2. Have you had a significant emotional experience that makes you aware you should be telling the story of salvation with others?

3. Discuss what constitutes successful evangelism.

4. Discuss how love can help an unbeliever over the stumbling block of the gospel.

5. Discuss the senior partner—junior partner relationship in the work of evangelism.

Activities:

1. Practice sharing the story of salvation using the five finger method described in the above section titled *God Provides the Message*.

2. Mark your Bible with a highlighter so you can easily find the following verses of Scripture: John 3:16, Romans 3:23, Ephesians 2:8, Romans 5:8, Romans 10:9-10.

Chapter 5

Conclusion

The four laymen found in Acts 6-10 describe how ordinary Christians can have a significant impact by sharing Jesus with those in their sphere of influence. These laymen provide an example of how people can make a significant contribution to evangelism.

Let's review what we have learned. First, we examined Stephen's story in Acts 6. Stephen taught us that character counts. If your life does not match your message, no one is going to listen to what you have to say. Conversely, if you live a life worthy of Christ, people will want to know what you have to say. Stephen also taught us that we will all face challenges when we tell the story of salvation. In the face of that challenge, however, Stephen taught us to make a clear, concise, and compelling case. Finally, Stephen demonstrated courage in the face of opposition.

Evangel-lies

Stephen's life taught us to not buy into three of Satan's worst lies. Stephen taught us to exert our influence for Christ, to not back down when Satan tries to persecute us, and to know what to say by learning a simple plan of salvation.

Second, Philip taught us that not everyone would be saved by the same method of evangelism. God uses different kinds of evangelism to reach different kinds of people. The Bible describes how Philip did mass evangelism in Samaria, church evangelism in the gathering of believers, and relationship evangelism with the Ethiopian eunuch.

We applied Philip's life story by exposing three more of Satan's lies. We learned from Scripture that evangelism is not just the job of the pastor. Everyone is responsible for sharing the story of salvation. We also learned that evangelism is not just supposed to be practiced in a program. Evangelism is a way of life. Finally, we learned that we all know people who are without Christ. We were challenged to not be people that neglect relationships with non-Christians. We learned to invite nonbelievers into our lives so that God can use us to share the story of salvation with them.

Third, Ananias taught us two principles. First, God intervenes in people's lives through their mind, memories, conscience, and spirit. Second, we learned that God wants believers involved in nonbelievers' lives. He wants us to identify with them. He wants us to identify His work for them. He wants us to identify their spiritual needs.

Ananias also taught us to face down three additional lies. He taught us to overcome our fear, take advantage of the doors of opportunity that God has given us, and have faith in God that He can do miracles to change people's lives.

Fourth, Cornelius taught us about God's work in evangelism. Many times Christians feel like they are going it alone. We learned that God prepares the hearer and the spokesman and that He also provides the message and produces the response. Christians are not going it alone when it comes to evangelism. God is right there, and He is involved.

Cornelius taught us the final three lies Satan tries to get Christians to believe. He taught us not to think of success and failure in worldly terms. Instead, he taught us to have a biblical concept of success and failure about evangelism. He also taught us that the gospel itself is offensive. While Christians do not seek to offend people, we must recognize that the gospel is a step on which many people stumble. Christians seek to help unbelievers over that step by loving them. Finally, we learned that God is going to reach people regardless of our obedience or disobedience. God is a saving, rescuing God. He desires for believers to be involved, but the question is about our obedience, not about God's saving work.

John 8:42-45 says, "Jesus said to them, If God were your Father, you would love me, for I came from God and now am here. I have not come on my own; but he sent me. Why is my language not clear to you? Because you are unable to hear what I say. You belong to your father, the devil, and you want

Evangel-lies

to carry out your father's desire. He was a murderer from the beginning, not holding to the truth, for there is no truth in him. When he lies, he speaks his native language, for he is a liar and the father of lies. Yet because I tell the truth, you do not believe me!"

Satan is a liar. The problem is that too many Christians are listening to his lies. We believe the lies he is promoting about evangelism. This book has been about teaching ordinary Christians about the impact their life, testimony, and witness can have when they reject the lies of Satan and obey the word of God.

God is a God of truth. His Word is true. His promises are true. His character is true. Christians must reject the lies and embrace the truth. God has taught us to tell the story of salvation. We can do nothing less than bring glory to Him by lovingly obeying.

I hope you have found in this book sufficient biblical insight to assist you in your personal Bible study. I also hope the real-life examples of these four witnesses have encouraged you to tell the story of salvation. I pray the personal stories have inspired you to share the story of salvation with those you know. I hope the biblical outlines will help you share with others the challenging message found in the book of Acts that exhorts believers to share the story of salvation.

Bibliography

—⚞—

Barclay, William. *The Acts of the Apostles Revised Edition*. Philadelphia: The Westminster Press, 1976.

Coleman, Robert E. *The Master Plan of Evangelism*. Grand Rapids: Fleming H. Revell Company, 1993.

Graham, Billy. *How to Be Born Again*. Dallas: Word Publishing, 1989.

Kennedy, D. James. *Evangelism Explosion*. Wheaton: Tyndale House Publishers, 1983.

Kistemaker, Simon J. *New Testament Commentary: Exposition of the Acts of the Apostles*. Grand Rapids: Baker Book House, 1990.

MacArthur, John. *The MacArthur New Testament Commentary: Acts 1-12*. Chicago: Moody Press, 1994.

Packer, J.I. *Evangelism and the Sovereignty of God.* Downers Grove: Illinois, 1961.

Pippert, Rebecca Manley. *Out of the Salt-Shaker and Into the World.* Downers Grove: Illinois, 1979.

Stott, John. *The Spirit, the Church and the World: The Message of Acts.* Downers Grove, Illinois, 1990.

Printed in the United States
75609LV00001B/169-1500